## Praise for
### *30 Days in the Land of the Psalms*

What wonderful insights greet us when we view the Psalms in their historical and cultural context! Charlie sheds light on these writings, which were inspired by God, but grew out of real-life situations in a particular time and place in history. I was edified and blessed!

**ERWIN W. LUTZER**
Pastor Emeritus
The Moody Church, Chicago

Few people have a grip on the Bible and the land of Israel like Charlie Dyer. He has the ability to both unearth the truths of the Psalms and skillfully connect them to locations in the Holy Land. If you are taking a trip to Israel soon, don't forget to pack this book. If you are not taking a trip to Israel soon, don't read this book—for it will create a yearning to visit that amazing land that will not be satisfied until you do.

**J. PAUL NYQUIST**
President, Moody Bible Institute

The heart of the Bible is the book of Psalms. It's the place we run to find comfort and understanding when life activates our emotions. I have a well-worn path to this special book of songs. But Charlie Dyer's *30 Days in the Land of the Psalms* opened this beloved hymnal for me like never before. The beauty of each psalm is magnified exponentially once you understand the background that led to its writing in the first place. After you go on this journey with Charlie, you'll have a deeper, and richer, understanding of the heart of God as seen through the majestic book of ages—the book of Psalms.

**TOM DOYLE**
Vice President and Middle East Director, e3 Partners
Author of *Standing in the Fire: Courageous Christians Living in Frightening Times* and *Killing Christians: Living the Faith Where It's Not Safe to Believe*

Charlie Dyer has an amazing grasp not only of the Scriptures, but also the Fifth Gospel—the land of Israel. With this keen insight, he powerfully presents a fresh perspective on many well-known and loved psalms. I highly recommend this resource. I know you will be both encouraged and challenged as you gain fresh insights into familiar psalms.

**DANN SPADER**
President, Global Youth Initiative
Founder, Sonlife Ministries

Many Christians read the Psalms every day but miss the fullness of their message. Why? The psalmists were poets, weaving images from the lands around them into the lines of Holy Scripture. Without a picture of what the Judean Wilderness looks like, or Masada, or the Mount of Olives, we read the words but miss so much of the message. Charlie Dyer is one of the most gifted expositors of the Holy Land I've ever read. As you read *30 Days in the Land of the Psalms*, you will picture the places of the poets. This book will help you do more than merely read the Psalms. *You'll see them.*

**WAYNE STILES**
Author, *Waiting on God*

The Psalms come alive in this practical portrait of the songs of Israel using the land of Israel as a canvas. Bible teacher and Israel expert Charlie Dyer provides a life-transforming exposition of the Psalms. Read it and heed it and get ready for God's Word to change your life.

**MICHAEL RYDELNIK**
Professor of Jewish Studies, Moody Bible Institute
Host, *Open Line with Dr. Michael Rydelnik*, Moody Radio

Charlie Dyer loves the Bible and loves the land of Israel. Both of these loves are powerfully brought together in this excellent book. I will use it whenever I study or teach the Psalms.

**MARK HITCHCOCK**
Senior Pastor, Faith Bible Church, Edmond, OK
Associate Professor of Bible Exposition, Dallas Theological Seminary

Charlie Dyer has the unique gift of communicating deep and wonderful truths in a few words. Those words open our eyes to new vistas of the biblical landscape and tune our ears to the voice of God calling to us in the wilderness of life. Each day's portion leaves you yearning to read the next for a closer look at the people, places, and promises of the Psalms. *30 Days in the Land of the Psalms* takes us far beyond interesting facts and photos; it is a pathway to an encounter with God in the midst of life's realities. This is one book that is destined to be a well-worn companion as its readers are enriched and encouraged time and time again.

**CLARENCE JOHNSON**
Director, The Institute of Jewish Studies, The Friends of Israel Gospel Ministry

For the best tour of the Holy Land, you need the right guide. In this virtual tour through the biblical land of the Psalms, Charlie Dyer is a trustworthy guide, providing sound Bible teaching backed by his immense knowledge of modern and ancient Israel. He provides a feast for the senses as he leads the reader from Mount Hermon through the arid wilderness and up to Jerusalem. This beautiful companion will open up the Psalms to readers in many fresh and delightful ways.

**TODD BOLEN**
Professor of Biblical Studies, The Master's University
Photographer, BiblePlaces.com

Having traveled to Israel and walked side by side with Charlie through the Holy Land, this book feels remarkably like . . . traveling to Israel and walking side by side with Charlie through the Holy Land! Though he lacks neither PhD nor pedigree, Charlie is always conversational and warm. And because he believes that a picture really is worth a thousand words, he has thoughtfully included photographs that are not just eye candy. They make you say, "Aha! So *this* is what the psalmist really meant."

**JON GAUGER**
Co-host, *The Land and the Book*, Moody Radio

For many years I have traveled to the Holy Land with Charlie. On every trip I have obtained a deeper understanding in correlating the Word with the intentional and artistic manner in which the Lord formed His Land. One thing becomes eminently clear in Charlie's *30 Days in the Land of the Psalms* . . . the magnificent connection between the songs of the temple hymnal and the land, which draws readers closer to the heart of God! Thank you, Charlie, for not only helping me understand the physical relationship between the Psalms and the land but also the personal perspective of a more intimate relationship with our Lord.

### GREG HATTEBERG
Dean of Enrollment and Alumni Services, Dallas Theological Seminary

The ultimate experience when reading the Psalms, in my opinion, is to read them early in the morning while looking over some part of the land of Israel where the psalm might have been written or where you can see something the psalm references. However, if you can't manage to do this, the next best thing would be to use *30 Days in the Land of the Psalms* by my good friend Charlie Dyer as your companion. Using his vast experience in the land of Israel and his insightful study in the Psalms, Charlie has allowed me to virtually be in Israel as I have read this wonderful devotional book. You too will be blessed, encouraged, instructed, and gain a greater appreciation of the reality of the Psalms as you use this helpful guide.

### STEPHEN J. BRAMER
Chair and Professor of Bible Exposition, Dallas Theological Seminary

In his virtual tour of the world of the Psalms, Charles Dyer does what he does best, introducing his "tourists" to the deeper content of Scripture in the context of the land of the Bible. If you love the Psalms, you will find here a new appreciation of old truths and a greater devotion to the Lord whose Word first came to His chosen people in a chosen place.

### J. RANDALL PRICE
Distinguished Research Professor, Liberty University

A HOLY LAND DEVOTIONAL

# 30 DAYS
# IN THE LAND
# *of the* Psalms

CHARLES H. DYER

**MOODY PUBLISHERS**
CHICAGO

All Scripture quotations, unless otherwise indicated, are taken from the New American Standard Bible®, Copyright © 1960, 1962, 1963, 1968, 1971, 1972, 1973, 1975, 1977, 1995 by The Lockman Foundation. Used by permission. (www.Lockman.org)

Scripture quotations marked KJV are taken from the King James Version.

Scripture quotations marked NKJV are taken from the New King James Version. Copyright © 1982 by Thomas Nelson. Used by permission. All rights reserved.

Scripture quotations marked NRSV are from the New Revised Standard Version of the Bible, copyright 1989, by the Division of Christian Education of the National Council of the Churches of Christ in the USA. Used by permission. All rights reserved.

Scripture quotations marked NIV are taken from the Holy Bible, New International Version®, NIV®. Copyright © 1973, 1978, 1984, 2011 by Biblica, Inc.™ Used by permission of Zondervan. All rights reserved worldwide. www.zondervan.com. The "NIV" and "New International Version" are trademarks registered in the United States Patent and Trademark Office by Biblica, Inc.™

All photographs are used by permission of Charles H. Dyer, the author.

Edited by Jim Vincent
Cover and interior design: Erik M. Peterson
Cover photo of antique paper copyright (c) 2015 by Geerati/iStock (478755306). All rights reserved.
Cover photo of grapevine courtesy of Unsplash.
Author photo: Jon Gauger

Library of Congress Cataloging-in-Publication Data

Names: Dyer, Charles H., 1952- author.
Title: 30 days in the land of the Psalms : a Holy Land devotional / Charles H
   Dyer.
Other titles: Thirty days in the land of the Psalms
Description: Chicago : Moody Publishers, 2017. | Includes bibliographical
   references.
Identifiers: LCCN 2016058996 (print) | LCCN 2017005151 (ebook) | ISBN
   9780802415691 | ISBN 9780802495549
Subjects: LCSH: Bible. Psalms--Meditations. | Palestine--Miscellanea.
Classification: LCC BS1430.54 .D94 2017 (print) | LCC BS1430.54 (ebook) | DDC
   242/.5--dc23
LC record available at https://lccn.loc.gov/2016058996

ISBN: 978-0-8024-1569-1

We hope you enjoy this book from Moody Publishers. Our goal is to provide high-quality, thought-provoking books and products that connect truth to your real needs and challenges. For more information on other books and products written and produced from a biblical perspective, go to www.moodypublishers.com or write to:

Moody Publishers
820 N. LaSalle Boulevard
Chicago, IL 60610

1 3 5 7 9 10 8 6 4 2

*Printed in the United States of America*

*To Cheri and Mike Fitzsimmons*
*and all the staff of Morning Star Tours—*
*friends who share my passion for Israel and who*
*work tirelessly to help others experience that*
*same life-changing reality.*
*Thank you for your commitment to excellence!*

*I was glad when they said to me,*
*"Let us go to the house of the L*ORD.*"*
*Our feet are standing within your gates, O Jerusalem.*
Psalm 122:1–2

# CONTENTS

# Introduction

In his commentary on the book of Psalms, American pastor and writer Warren Wiersbe described this collection of songs as "the irreplaceable devotional guide, prayer book, and hymnal of the people of God."[1] We all have our own favorite passages in the book of Psalms—from individual verses to entire psalms—to which we often turn for comfort, consolation, and hope in our journey through life. But how much do we really know about these songs of faith we love so much?

Unfortunately, in many cases we know very little. The passages we cherish are like small thumbnail portraits cropped from their larger geographical and historical context. We admire their beauty but know little about their backgrounds. And as a result we often miss the greater depth and richness those passages have to offer.

For example, in Psalm 23 David reminds us that the

Lord is our shepherd. But what was it like to shepherd a flock of sheep in the desolate Judean Wilderness? To someone living in the United States, green pastures and still waters might call to mind a manicured park alongside a placid lake, but what was David envisioning when he wrote those words? It's only as we stumble our way across jagged rocks on the edge of a steep ravine dotted with small tufts of shriveled, brown grass that we begin to understand the psalmist's words in a deeper, richer way.

Traveling to Israel provides insight into the book of Psalms by allowing a pilgrim to examine more closely the individual canvases on which each of the 150 masterpieces were painted. And that's why I encourage everyone who possibly can to visit the Holy Land. But I do recognize that many, perhaps most, will never have that opportunity. That's one reason for writing this devotional guide. My goal is to take you on a *virtual* tour to Israel—to help you see the land in a way that allows you to read this section of God's Word with greater clarity and insight. Our trip will explore the landscape that forms the backdrop to the Psalms. To help visualize the scenes being painted by the writers I've included photographs from my various tours of the Holy Land.

I invite you to join me on a trip to the land of Kings Saul, David, and Solomon, and all the other writers who contributed to God's songbook we know as the book of Psalms.

For the next thirty days I want us to explore the land while holding the book of Psalms in our hand. We won't cover all the psalms, but we will explore enough to give you a sense of walking through the wilderness with David and the other psalmists, traveling to Jerusalem with the throngs of pilgrims, and hiking the mountains of the land—from Mount Hermon on Israel's northern border to the Mount of Olives, from which throngs of pilgrims first caught sight of Jerusalem and the Temple! For those who have already traveled to Israel, I hope this book brings back wonderful memories of your life-changing time in the land.

Before we begin our journey, let's take a quick overview of the book itself. Most Christians love reading from the book of Psalms, but few have ever really studied how the book was put together. They view it as 150 different songs, much like the individual hymns in a hymnbook. But the book of Psalms has a very definite arrangement. It's actually divided into five books or collections. Psalms 1–41 are Book 1, and they are mostly a collection of psalms written by David. Then, if you look closely in your Bible, you will discover Psalms 42–72 are labeled as Book 2, and so on through the entire collection. These books help identify the process by which the individual psalms were collected and added to the Bible.

Each of the five books or collections also ends with a separate blessing or benediction. For example, Psalm 41 ends by saying, "Blessed be the LORD, the God of Israel, from everlasting to everlasting. Amen and Amen" (v. 13). And Psalm 72 ends in a similar fashion: "Blessed be the LORD God, the God of Israel, who alone works wonders. And blessed be His glorious name forever; and may the whole earth be filled with His glory. Amen, and Amen" (vv. 18–19). Each of the books, or collections of psalms, ends with a similar benediction—with the last five psalms serving as the benediction for the entire book.

While the overall structure of the book is fascinating, it's the message of each individual psalm that speaks to our hearts. Whether we're facing life's struggles or rejoicing in God's blessings, it seems we can always find a psalm that matches the mood of our spirit. And that's what makes the book of Psalms a songbook for all occasions.

*30 Days in the Land of the Psalms* is a one-month devotional guide that will take you on an extended journey to Israel . . . and into the book of Psalms. Our goal each day is to connect the land of Israel with the message of a specific psalm. Hopefully you will come to understand and appreciate both as we travel together.

But our ultimate goal is not simply to read God's Word. We want to move His truth from our heads to our hearts. As James wrote, "Do not merely listen to the word, and so deceive yourselves. Do what it says" (1:22 NIV). So grab your Bible, lace up your hiking boots, and follow me out into the land of Israel for a life-changing encounter with David and the psalmists!

# The One Who Is Blessed

## PSALM 1

Every January 1 we wish friends and loved ones a "Happy New Year!" But how would you like to go one step better next year and have a *blessed* New Year? The difference in wording might sound slight, but the change in our lives can be profound. To see what that change looks like, we need to head to Israel to visit the author of Psalm 1.

Psalm 1 was apparently *not* written by David. Instead, it serves as an introduction to the entire book of Psalms. If Psalms were a regular book, we would call Psalm 1 the foreword—the introduction that helps explain what the book is all about. We're not told who wrote the psalm, and that's okay because we know God is the ultimate Author.

Psalm 1 helps us see more clearly that there are only two roadways in life we can choose to follow. One leads to prosperity and blessing, the other to judgment and destruction.

And we're responsible for the pathway we choose.

In Israel, roads developed over time following the path of least resistance. Through trial and error people discovered the pathway with the least number of obstacles or that traveled the shortest distance. It's not that you couldn't try a different route, but doing so usually resulted in more difficulty and hardship.

And perhaps that's why the writer of Psalm 1 begins by picturing the two roadways available to each person journeying through life. He first announces to his readers that the person who is truly blessed is the one who chooses *not* to follow the roadway running counter to the plan and purpose of God. "How blessed is the man who does not walk in the counsel of the wicked, nor stand in the path of sinners, nor sit in the seat of scoffers!" (1:1).

Don't miss the progression. The person on this wrong pathway starts by listening to the counsel of those who don't follow God. The person then begins acting like those walking along that same pathway. And the final destination is a life that scornfully rejects all that God has said is right. But apparently this way of rebellion becomes progressively more treacherous. We find this traveler walking . . . then standing . . . and finally sitting or ceasing his journey altogether to make this place of scoffers his final destination. He might not have started out with this destination in mind, but it's where the pathway ultimately leads.

If that's the path leading to destruction, then what's the path that leads to blessing? The writer gives the answer in verse 2. The path of blessing is the path that leads to God's Word. The person who spends time in God's Word, finding pleasure in it and thinking through what God has said, is the person who discovers the pathway leading to God's blessing.

The writer then changes metaphors as he turns from the two pathways we can choose to focus on the two different destinations we'll reach. And he uses agricultural imagery to make his point. Those who choose to focus on and follow God's Word are like the fruit-bearing

A fig tree thriving along the edge of a stream.

trees in Israel that are fortunate enough to be "planted by streams of water" (1:3). They produce the proper results in the proper season, and when times of heat and drought come, they're connected to a source of nourishment that sustains them.

The psalmist's word picture was striking because of the relatively small number of streams in Israel. Most fruit-bearing trees in Bible times—whether date palms, figs, olives, or pomegranates—were *not* planted by streams of water, because such streams didn't flow through the plots of land owned by most farmers. Any farmer with a stream or other water source on his land was indeed fortunate! Water from such a stream would nourish his trees during the six months of every year when no rain falls on the land.

Stop and look closely at the fig tree next to us. It's early October, and it hasn't rained for nearly six months. Yet this tree is thriving. I would let you try one of the figs, but it looks like other visitors have already "harvested" all the ones in reach! While much of the land is brown and dry, why is this tree so full of life? The secret is the ever-flowing stream of water right next to its trunk.

The psalmist now turns to a second agricultural image to complete the sad contrast between the righteous and those now specifically identified as the wicked. Those who choose the other pathway will not experience the same results. Rather than being fruitful and nourished, they're as parched as the dry seed coverings that fall from the wheat. They have nothing of substance to hold them firm when the scorching winds of life blow in, nothing to keep them rooted and nourished. Like the "chaff which the wind drives" (v. 4) from the wheat, they have little of substance or value to hold them firm.

As the writer draws his comparison to a conclusion, he returns to where he began. The person who chooses the pathway of the wicked will *not* stand in the assembly of the righteous at the time of God's divine judgment. That's the time when God will eternally separate the wheat from the chaff.

In contrast, God says that He "knows the way of the righteous" (v. 6). And the word for *know* has the idea of personal, intimate knowledge. The word is sometimes used as a euphemism for sexual relations between a man and a woman (Gen. 4:1). If you choose to follow the path of God, you not only come to know God, but you discover He also knows you in a deep, personal way. Sadly, the other pathway leads only to heartache, loss, and ruin.

**WALKING IN OUR LAND**

**SO WHAT'S THE LESSON** for us as we begin this thirty-day journey into the book of Psalms? Let me offer two practical suggestions, each based on the two pathways available to us. Do you want to discover God's blessing in your life through this study, to come to know Him in a deep, personal, and intimate way? Then resolve right now to begin reading and meditating on His Word every day. You'll discover a living source of blessing that will sustain and nourish you through whatever may come your way in the coming weeks.

But as you start this study, what if you realize you've been walking down the wrong pathway of life? The good news is that it's never too late to return to God. Psalm 103:11b–13 says, "Great is His lovingkindness toward those who fear Him. As far as the east is from the west, so far has He removed our transgressions from us. Just as a father has compassion on his children, so the LORD has compassion on those who fear Him." Why not make this the moment when you begin a personal relationship with God? Place your trust in Jesus as your personal Savior, your Deliverer from sin who brings you to a forgiving Father. Then find a church that believes and teaches the Bible where you can go and learn more about this pathway to spiritual blessing that God has available for you!

# What Can the Righteous Do?

## Psalm 11

One of my favorite places in Israel is the Mount of Olives with its sweeping view of Jerusalem. We'll return to this spot several times during our time together in the psalms. As we step off the bus, try to follow me through the mass of people—and peddlers! Don't get distracted by the postcards, panoramic posters, bookmarks, "genuine" pashmina shawls, or offers of a camel ride. Instead, walk with me to a spot where we can look out over the city of Jerusalem. Now, crowd together to keep out the peddlers, and turn on your headset so you can hear me above the din of the crowd.

As we stand here on the summit of the Mount of Olives, in front of us is Jerusalem and the golden Dome of the Rock, one of the most iconic buildings in the world. But I want you to mentally erase all the buildings, and the platform on which they rest and try to envision this scene as it would have looked in the time of David. The Dome of the Rock rests on Mount Moriah. In David's day a threshing floor stood on top of that mount. And Jerusalem, the City of David, wasn't the large city you see in front of you today.

Look to the left of the platform. See that tiny slice of land outside the walls of today's Old City? That's the original fortified city of Jebus, the place David captured and made his capital.

Now, imagine David standing down there, just outside the city walls, with a small group of advisers. We can't quite hear what they're saying from this distance, so let's

View of Jerusalem from the Mount of Olives.

walk down the Mount of Olives and across the Kidron Valley to join the group. As we approach, we see David's agitated advisers waving their arms and pointing toward the spot where we had just been standing.

"Your majesty, the enemy is approaching from the south and west! Your only hope of escape is to flee over the Mount of Olives into the wilderness. Hurry to the mountain while you still have time to escape!"

We've arrived at a time of panic and indecision. David's life is being threatened, and his frightened advisers see only one course of action. Run! Get out! Head to the safety of some remote hideout! We're not told the

specific threat, but it's obviously a time of danger and fear . . . and uncertainty. And in the middle of these panicked advisers stands David *calmly;* he is writing on a piece of parchment. Our curiosity gets the best of us, and we walk over to see what he's writing. As we read his words we recognize Psalm 11, a psalm of David.

The first verse reflects the response of David to the panicked words of his advisers. "In the LORD I take refuge; how can you say to my soul, 'Flee as a bird to your mountain.'" David's advisers were normally very wise and prudent. What had them so afraid that they wanted David to run for his life? In the next two verses David relays his counselors' words of panic. "For, behold, the wicked bend the bow, they make ready their arrow upon the string to shoot in darkness at the upright in heart. If the foundations are destroyed, what can the righteous do?" (11:2–3).

Their words were of fear and warning. They may also have said, "David, the wicked are ready and able to attack without warning. Your life is in mortal danger. If they kill you, they will take over the kingdom. Your only hope is to run, now!"

But instead of glancing nervously over his shoulder, or becoming as agitated as his advisors, David calmly lifts his eyes toward heaven. And then he begins writing as he speaks to his advisers, recording the words as they come from his mouth. "The LORD is in His holy temple; the LORD's throne is in heaven; His eyes behold, His eyelids test the sons of men" (v. 4). The enemy might be somewhere just outside the city, but God is still seated calmly on His throne in heaven—and nothing takes the God of heaven by surprise.

David reminds his advisers that God knows how to deal with both the righteous and the wicked. "The LORD tests the righteous and the wicked" (v. 5). The word for *test* has the idea of examining or scrutinizing. God is not only omnipotent, seated on His heavenly throne. David reminds his frightened advisers that God is also omniscient. He can examine and scrutinize everything going on. Nothing escapes His gaze!

God is omnipotent and omniscient, but David also finds a calmness in the middle of chaos by reminding himself that God is also just and righteous. He's a God who will judge evil and reward the upright. "And the one who loves violence His soul hates. Upon the wicked He will rain snares; fire and brimstone and burning wind will be the portion of their cup. For the LORD is righteous, He loves righteousness; the upright will behold His face" (vv. 5b–7). David refuses to panic because he could trust in the character of God as a righteous judge.

The wicked thought they were going to trap and kill David. But David knows that in reality they were going to be entrapped by God. God would pour down snares on them like rain, traps that they could not see and would not expect. Changing metaphors, David pictured God sending down on the wicked the raging heat of fiery coals and burning sulfur, an allusion to the sudden and complete destruction God brought on Sodom and Gomorrah.

How can David be so confident? His confidence rested in the absolute character of God. God was Himself just and righteous. We rightly view God as a God of love. But David also describes Him as a God who "hates" those who embrace violence and wickedness. The word for *hate* has the idea of being unable or unwilling to put up with something, to the point of being an enemy. God has great affection for those who trust Him and seek to follow Him, but God will violently oppose those who rebel against His ways and seek to harm His followers. David remained calm in the midst of chaos because he understood the essential character of the God he served.

**WALKING IN OUR LAND**

**AS WE TURN TO BEGIN** our climb back up the Mount of Olives, what lesson can we take away from David's words of calm assurance in Psalm 11? Perhaps we can begin by looking at the parallels between our own day and the troubles facing David. We're shocked and dismayed by world events in which the wicked seem to run roughshod over those powerless to stop them. We see evil leaders growing in power and influence, while those who try to stand for God's standards of right and wrong are ridiculed and marginalized. It's enough to make us want to flee like a bird to some mountain hideout!

But don't give in to panic or fear. Instead, remember the three truths about God from Psalm 11 that kept David stable in otherwise unstable times. God is still on His throne. He's *omnipotent;* He has all power. God also sees everything taking place in the world. He's *omniscient;* He knows everything. And God is still the righteous judge who will, in His time, judge the wicked and demonstrate His love and blessing to the righteous. He is just. Count on it!

# God Is My Masada

## PSALM 18

Masada is the desert fortress built by Herod the Great. Stark. Imposing. A seemingly impenetrable palace built atop a 1,200-foot mesa, it towers over the Dead Sea, with cliffs on every side. And as if the cliffs didn't offer enough protection, Herod ringed the citadel with walls and stored up weapons and supplies that he thought would be sufficient to repel all attacks.

Masada was Herod's security blanket, his refuge of last resort should his greatest fears ever come to pass. And he had a lot to fear! Josephus, the ancient Jewish historian, described Herod's obsession with Masada this way: "Herod furnished this fortress as a refuge for himself against two kinds of danger: peril on the one hand from the Jewish people, lest they should depose him and restore their former dynasty to power. The greater and more serious threat was from Cleopatra, queen of

Egypt. For she never concealed her intentions, but was constantly begging Anthony, urging him to kill Herod, and confer on her the throne of Judea."[1]

Constant fear of an uprising on the part of those he ruled. Threats from Cleopatra of Egypt, coupled with a realization of how much influence she had in Rome. Herod must have slept lightly because of these grave dangers. Little wonder he was obsessed with making Masada the most secure palace in all the Middle East. This was his doomsday fortress.

Herod put his trust in Masada. It became his hope for protection, his insurance policy for survival should he ever lose his grip on power. He didn't give the site its name, but in Hebrew the name Masada, *metsudah*, means "fortress" or "stronghold." And the name certainly matched Herod's confidence in the location. It was the strongest, most defensible, most secure site in all the land.

Less than eighty years after Herod's death, Masada's invincibility was put to the test. And sadly, its final defenders discovered that any stronghold built with human hands can eventually be conquered. Masada fell to the Roman army in AD 73, ending the first Jewish revolt against Rome. Masada was the last fortress in Judea to fall . . . but it *did* fall. Today tourists can hike up the high mesa by following the original "Snake Path" on the side facing the Dead Sea or by walking up a path along the Roman siege ramp to the west. But the easy way to the top is by an aerial tramway that whisks passengers from the Visitors Center to near the top in only three minutes.

Herod is the one who made the site into a doomsday fortress, while Rome's attack—and the mass suicide of its Jewish defenders—helped make the site famous. Yet Herod wasn't the first to notice the strategic advantage of Masada. In fact, David walked across the summit of this mesa a thousand years before Herod. And the name given to this rocky plateau—*metsudah*, the stronghold— preceded even David.

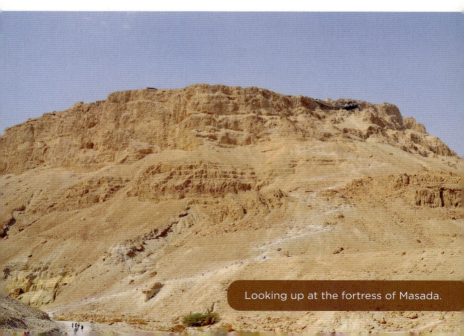

Looking up at the fortress of Masada.

In 1 Samuel 22 we catch a glimpse of young David as a fugitive from King Saul. He's a man on the run, pursued by a jealous king bent on killing anyone he saw as a potential rival to the throne. After hiding in the cave of Adullam in Judah's western foothills, David and his band of followers went to Bethlehem to rescue David's parents from potential harm and to carry them safely to Moab, on the eastern side of the Dead Sea. Why Moab? Perhaps because it was the home country of David's great-grandmother Ruth, the Moabitess. David hoped his family would be safe in the care of distant relatives and outside the clutches of King Saul.

As he crossed back over the Dead Sea, returning from Moab, David looked for a hideout in the Judean desert, a place where he could be safe from attack. Perhaps even a location with a remarkable view in all directions, one that would not allow Saul to sneak up on him undetected. So where did he go? First Samuel 22:4 says David went to "the stronghold." The word in Hebrew is *metsudah*, Masada. Evidently, it was the name for this mesa even in David's day.

From a human perspective Masada seemed like the perfect hideout. But it's not where God wanted David to stay. The prophet Gad received a message from God. "Do not stay in the stronghold; depart and go into the land of Judah" (1 Sam. 22:5). David obeyed God and climbed down from Masada. But just a few chapters later he was back.

David's final encounter with Saul took place at En Gedi, the spring of the wild goats, just ten miles north of Masada. After the encounter, Saul and his army went northwest toward Saul's capital at Gibeah. How much did David trust Saul's promise not to harm him? Well, as Saul turned and marched north, David headed south. First Samuel 24:22 says it this way. "And Saul went to his home, but David and his men went up to the stronghold." David went to *metsudah*, Masada. This was an excellent place where David could watch and see if Saul might "change his mind" and double back to try to catch David off guard. From the northern edge of Masada, David had an excellent view all the way back to En Gedi.

At first glance we might not be surprised that both David and Herod discovered the strategic advantages of a location like Masada. Both men faced military threats during their lives, and both came to appreciate the importance of a strong defensive position. But that's where the similarities end. Herod trusted in his military might, including fortresses like Masada. He didn't live long enough to learn that even this fortress would fail.

Unlike Herod, David trusted in God for protection.

How do we know this? David wrote Psalm 18 to commemorate God's promised protection "in the day that the LORD delivered him from the hand of all his enemies and from the hand of Saul." David began with a summary statement of God's great protection. "The LORD is my rock and my fortress and my deliverer, my God, my rock, in whom I take refuge; my shield and the horn of my salvation, my stronghold" (18:2). And guess what word David used for *fortress*? You're right! It's *metsudah*, Masada.

In Psalm 31 David makes a similar statement. He doesn't tell us the specific background for the psalm, but it was evidently written during a time of great difficulty when even David's friends abandoned him. He pleads with God to be "a rock of strength, a stronghold to save me" (31:2). One verse later David declares with confidence, "For You are my rock and my fortress." Unlike Herod, David didn't depend on a doomsday fortress when he faced times of trouble. His *metsudah*, his fortress, was the living God!

**WALKING IN OUR LAND**

**LIKE DAVID AND LIKE HEROD,** we all experience times when we feel threatened by circumstances beyond our control. When those difficult times come, what's your stronghold? Where do you ultimately turn for help? Herod looked to Masada and saw a physical fortress that seemed safe, almost impregnable. But history ultimately proved him wrong. David spent time on the same mesa, but he came to a radically different conclusion. David found his protection not in *metsudah*, but in the Rock of Ages, the living fortress, God Almighty.

Whether you go to Israel and visit Masada or simply refer to the enclosed photograph, take a moment to look up at the summit—and then realize how much greater is the God of the universe.

Finally, open Psalm 18 and focus on the true *metsudah*. "The LORD is my rock and my fortress and my deliverer. . . . I call upon the LORD, who is worthy to be praised, and I am saved from my enemies" (18:2–3).

# Facing the Future with Confidence

## PSALM 20

Most of us face the future with a mixture of antici- pation and anxiety. No matter our age or stage in life, many of us find ourselves wondering, what lies over the horizon? Will the coming months and years bring health and happiness . . . or heartache?

In the haunting wedding song from the Broadway musical *Fiddler on the Roof,* "Sunrise, Sunset," Tevye and his wife marvel at how quickly life has passed, and how each season comes "laden with happiness and tears." It's virtually certain that you will experience your own share of both happiness and tears in the coming months. And that's why Psalm 20 is so strategic. It can help us face the future with calmness and confidence.

Now, when you first read this psalm, you might be confused as you notice the psalm focusing on an im- pending battle. But it's the uncertainty of what lies in the future that is the common thread that makes this psalm, and prayer, so applicable to all our lives today.

The psalm begins in verse 1 with the people praying for their king, who is about to lead them into battle. "May the Lord answer you in the day of trouble! May the name of the God of Jacob set you securely on high!" From a human perspective the future *is* uncertain. Battles can be won or lost by events beyond the most capable leader's control. But nothing is beyond God's control, so the people pray and ask God to *answer* and *protect* their king as he goes into battle.

Recognizing that God is the one ultimately in control is the key to this prayer for an uncertain future. Speaking to the king, the people ask God to "grant you your heart's desire and fulfill all your counsel" (20:4). We can plan, but it's God who can bring our plans to completion . . . or to ruin. Recognizing the need for God's help and intervention is crucial.

Verse 6 is a response to this prayer. The Psalm moves from "we" to "I," from the group to one individual. Some believe it's a priest responding to the group. I think it might be the response of King David himself. In either case, the person, after listening to the heartfelt prayers of the people, responds with confidence. "Now I know that the Lord saves His anointed; He will answer him from His holy heaven with the saving strength of His right hand."

The prayer in verse 1 was for God to answer and protect. In verse 6 the leader affirms his confidence in God's ability to do just that. Reversing the order he says he knows God will *save*, or deliver, His anointed and will *answer* from heaven.

But how can the people, or the leader, have such confidence? After all, the future is still, well, the future! It hasn't yet happened. What is it that can give them such confidence about events that are still over the horizon? The answer is found in verse 7. "Some boast in chariots and some in horses, but we will boast in the name of the LORD, our God." This verse in Hebrew is really quite interesting. It literally says, "These in chariots, and these in horses, but we in the name of the LORD our God will remember."

The word we translate *boast* is really the Hebrew word for "remember," *zachar*. The particular form of the word here has the idea of mentioning, or reminding, or causing someone to remember. It's not so much boasting about something as it is reminding people of what they have. Boasting suggests arrogance, and I don't see any arrogance in what's being said here. When trouble comes, some people like to look around to see what they have

An Israeli tank, the present-day equivalent of a chariot, on the Golan Heights.

that can take care of them. Some point to their physical resources, their chariots and horses, for example. But as we look around, we can remind people that we have the covenant-keeping God of the universe on our side!

Having reminded the listeners of the different sources of strength on which the two sides depend, the leader now shares the results of depending on each one. What happens to those who place their trust in chariots and horses? "They have bowed down and fallen" (20:8a). David might have in mind Judges 4, where Israel faced an army that had nine hundred iron chariots. Going into the battle, it looked as if those with the horses and chariots had an insurmountable advantage. But then God brought a cloudburst just as the battle began—and all the chariots got stuck in the mud! That's when the forces under Barak charged down from Mount Tabor to win a decisive victory!

Those who trust in mere human ability bow down and fall, but those who remember—and depend on—God "have risen and stood upright" (20:8b). The prophet Zechariah's name comes from this same Hebrew word, *zachar*. His name means "The Lord remembers." And he emphasizes essentially the same truth in his message to Judah's rulers in his day. "'Not by might nor by power, but by My Spirit,' says the LORD of hosts" (Zech. 4:6). God would complete what He had promised to do, no matter how strong the opposition, or obstacles, might seem.

The psalmist ends his prayer by repeating the same request he had at the very beginning. "Save, O LORD; may the King answer us in the day we call" (v. 9). God is in control, but we still need to come to Him in prayer and ask for His help. The identity of the "king" mentioned in this verse is uncertain. Some believe it refers to David, and they translate the verse as a request by the people for God to spare King David. But it's also possible that the king they have in mind is God Himself (thus the capital K in "king" in the NASB). When they cry, "May the King answer us in the day we call," they could be calling on God, as the ultimate King, to answer. And I like that perspective because it seems to fit best with the psalm. David is acknowledging that even the human king has to trust in the King of kings as he looks toward the future.

**WALKING IN OUR LAND**

**SO WHAT HAVE WE DISCOVERED** in Psalm 20 that can help us face our own future? How about this: We don't know what lies just over the horizon, but God does. It's so easy to depend on those things we can see and touch and feel, like the chariots and horses in David's day—or our bank account and 401(k) today. But as we pray for God's guidance through tomorrow's uncharted waters, the most important truth we need to remember, to rely on almost to the point of boasting, is that *God* is the one in charge. He knows what's ahead, and He's the one who can help us through our uncertain times.

Just remember: "Some boast in chariots and some in horses, but we will boast in the name of the Lord, our God" (20:7). And that might just make a pretty good New Year's resolution for January 1—or any other day of the year!

# Forsaken by God

## PSALM 22

Today we're going to visit three sites in rapid succession. And I want you to pay close attention because there will be a quiz at the end of our tour. Our first stop is on the Golan Heights in the far north of Israel. Bring along your jacket because the temperature can be a little cool. Depending on the time of year, you might even need your umbrella. But as you stand with me here on the rim of this extinct volcanic crater, I think you can see why I wanted to bring you here. Mount Hermon, the highest peak in all Israel, rises up just to our north in all its snow-capped glory. All around us the fields are a deep shade of green and dotted with purple, red, and yellow flowers. On our drive up we saw herds of large, well-fed cattle grazing on the lush green grass.

I know you would like to stay, but we need to hustle to our next stop, the so-called Citadel of David in Jeru-

salem. From the citadel's tower we have a picturesque
view of the Old City. There's the gold-clad Dome of the
Rock with the Mount of Olives just behind it. The white
limestone buildings glisten in the sun, and we sense the
vibrant energy of this amazing city. From our perch we
spot more cars than cows, but the open spaces we do see
are still green. Okay, now hustle down the steps because
we need to reach our final stop before the sun drops too
low on the horizon.

We arrived just in time! Sorry about the steep climb
up the rock-strewn hillside; be careful where you walk.
That chasm in front of you drops hundreds of feet before

*Left:* A solitary bull grazing on a hillside in the Golan
Heights. *Middle:* The Dome of the Rock and the Mount
of Olives from David's Citadel. *Right:* A deep ravine
carving its way through the Judean Wilderness.

reaching the valley floor. The hills are turning a golden brown as the sun drops toward the western horizon, sharpening the outlines of all the canyons carving their way into the barren rock. The one thing missing from this overlook is *green*. No plants. No grass. No flowers. Just dusty rocks and dirt.

Okay, now it's quiz time. Of the three spots we've visited, which one would you describe as "God forsaken"? A, B, or C? I have a feeling you voted for C. But based on Psalm 22, you're wrong! The answer is A or B! I see you're confused, so let's visit with David to see what he wrote in this psalm of personal distress.

In Psalm 22 David cries out to God for deliverance. And his opening words are some of the saddest in the entire Bible. "My God, my God, why have You forsaken me?" We talk about a *place* being God-forsaken, but David applies those words to a *person*. Historically he's describing himself, but God had him pen these words in a way that pointed forward prophetically to events associated with the life of Jesus. In fact, these are the very words Jesus cried from the cross during His crucifixion.

The parallels between David and Jesus wind through the entire psalm. Both found themselves "a reproach of men and despised by the people" (v. 6). And in perhaps the most dramatic scene of all, David announced that his enemies have "pierced my hands and my feet" (v. 16). What David felt symbolically, Jesus actually experienced. David's death was so certain his enemies were already plotting to divide up his possessions as spoils of victory. "They divide my garments among them, and for my clothing they cast lots" (v. 18). And, of course, this was literally fulfilled by the Roman soldiers overseeing Jesus' crucifixion on the cross.

But what does any of this have to do with the Golan Heights, Jerusalem, or the wilderness? Actually, quite a bit! First, the place where God's Anointed One was forsaken was Jerusalem. And second, David described his enemies as being like "strong bulls of Bashan" (v. 12). Bashan is the Old Testament name for the area we now call the Golan Heights. We appreciate Jerusalem and the Golan Heights for their beauty, but to David—at least in this psalm—they represent places associated with his persecutors.

In contrast, the wilderness was the place where David and Jesus found protection and deliverance. God delivered David from Saul in the wilderness. And God strengthened Jesus after His wilderness encounter with Satan.

All this brings us back to Psalm 22. Remember, the psalm identifies a person, not a place, as being forsaken by God. The ultimate fulfillment of David's heartfelt cry of abandonment was experienced in Jesus on the cross. But how could Jesus be forsaken by God? The apostle Paul provides the answer in 2 Corinthians 5:21. "[God] made Him who knew no sin to be sin on our behalf, so that we might become the righteousness of God in Him." As He hung on the cross, Jesus became *our* sin offering. He experienced punishment that rightly belonged to us.

But Psalm 22 ends in triumph, not despair. David compared his enemies to bulls (v. 12), lions (v. 13), dogs (v. 16a), and "a band of evildoers" who pierced his hands and feet (v. 16b). But then, in typical Hebrew fashion reversing the order, he cried out to God, "Deliver my soul from the *sword*, my only life from the power of the *dog*. Save me from the *lion's* mouth; from the horns of the *wild oxen* You answer me" (vv. 20–21, italics added).

When David began this heartfelt prayer, he felt forsaken by God and oppressed by his enemies. But his time in prayer gave him a new perspective. "For He has not despised nor abhorred the affliction of the afflicted; nor has He hidden His face from him; but when he cried to Him for help, He heard" (v. 24). Through prayer, David was able to look beyond his immediate problems and focus on God's promised solution—a solution that would also extend to future generations (v. 30).

**WALKING IN OUR LAND**

**WHAT PROBLEMS ARE YOU** facing today? Are you so overwhelmed that you feel as if even God has abandoned you? If so, read back through Psalm 22 . . . and remember that you're not alone. King David felt the same way. Slow down when you reach verse 19. Read David's heartfelt *cry* in verses 19–21, and then focus on his *confidence* in verses 22–31.

Linger over the last two verses. David announced that future generations "will declare His righteousness to a people who will be born, that He has performed it." Those people yet to be born included you! David wanted *you* to know God hasn't abandoned you. He *will* come to help just like He did for David—and for Jesus!

# The Good Shepherd

## PSALM 23:1–4

Let's take the next two days to look at what is perhaps the best-known of the psalms, the reassuring Psalm 23. Many can recite it, but few fully understand it. So we'll be trekking out into the Judean Wilderness—and then returning to the royal court—to look at this classic psalm of trust with fresh eyes. For today's journey, make sure your hiking shoes are firmly laced and your canteen is full . . . and then follow me into the wilderness!

One of my greatest adventures in Israel was an all-day hike through the Judean Wilderness. About an hour into that trip we rounded a bend in the gorge and came across a shepherdess tending a small flock of goats. She had positioned herself so she could keep a watchful eye on her flock as it grazed its way through brown tufts of dry grass and thorny shrubs in that otherwise desolate valley.

That young shepherdess reminded me of David watching over his flock in that same region three thousand years ago. Before his rise to prominence as Israel's king, before his victory over Goliath, before his appearance in King Saul's court as a musician—before all that, David's job was to watch over his father's flock in the wilderness. It was *here* that he became skillful in using a sling, and it was probably here where he honed his musical skills and composed songs that later found their way into the book of Psalms.

We're not sure when David penned Psalm 23, but the first four verses harken back to his time as a shepherd. You can almost hear the bleating of the flock in the background as David takes us into the wilderness to share the lessons he learned about God during this time of solitude.

"The LORD is my shepherd, I shall not want." The word for *shepherd* comes from a Hebrew root that means "to look upon" or "to watch over." A shepherd "watched over" the flock under his care. David began this psalm by affirming that God was the Shepherd watching over him. And with God as shepherd, the flock lacked nothing.

I remember being confused when I memorized Psalm 23 as a child. "The LORD is my shepherd; I shall not want." *But why wouldn't I* want *God to be my shepherd*, I thought. Later I learned that the word *want* really meant "to be in need." The shepherd's role was to make sure the flock had sufficient grass and water. Since *God* is the one watching over me, I can trust Him to meet my needs.

David illustrated his opening statement with two word pictures that look back to his time watching over the flock. How does a shepherd provide for his sheep? First, "He makes me lie down in green pastures" (23:2a). The word we translate "green" actually refers to new grass, the kind that sprouts when the winter rains arrive. It's succulent, moisture-rich, and tender, the most beneficial food for the flock.

His second word picture comes from the springs of water that dot the wilderness. "He leads me beside quiet waters" (23:2b). There were—and still are—relatively few springs in the wilderness, and it was the wise shepherd who knew their location. He could be trusted to lead his sheep to those sources of water. We think of "still waters"

*Left:* A shepherdess watching over her flock in the wilderness.
*Right:* Watching a flock of sheep grazing in green pastures.

as pools with little movement of the water, but that's not exactly what David says. It's not "still waters" but "waters of rest." David is picturing waters that are quiet, calming, and restful. Here the flock can drink in quiet safety, unafraid of any wild animals that might be lurking nearby, thanks to the shepherd's watchful eye.

So what happens when the good shepherd leads his flock to hillsides covered in sprouts of tender grass and to restful springs of water? "He restores my soul" (23:3a). The flock is *nourished* and *refreshed*. The hungry are satisfied; and the thirsty revived.

David then adds, "He guides me in the paths of righteousness for His name's sake" (23:3b). God's ways are good, because God Himself is good. Though we might not understand all that happens in our lives, we can be confident that the specific path on which He takes us is the right one because it's God's "name"—His very reputation—that is at stake.

The good shepherd nourishes and sustains the flock under his care. But his role involves more than just providing for the *physical* needs of the flock. He also guards the flock from danger. "Even though I walk through the valley of the shadow of death, I fear no evil, for You are with me" (23:4a). But what is the "valley of the shadow of death"?

There are two words in Hebrew to describe valleys. One evokes a broad, wide valley, the other, a steep, narrow valley. Here, David used the word for the narrow valley, which perfectly describes the deep gorges that cut through the Judean Wilderness. The phrase "shadow of death" is really just a single Hebrew word that occurs seventeen times in the Old Testament. Jeremiah used it to describe the Sinai desert as a "land of drought and of *deep darkness*" (Jer. 2:6, italics added). And in the Book of Job it was used nine times to characterize the place of the dead. But what is David describing?

I believe David used the deep valley of darkness to represent life's dangers. As night fell, dark shadows crept through the deep valleys of the Judean Wilderness. The darkness hid a multitude of dangers from the unwary flock. Wild animals left their dens to prowl for unsuspecting prey. Death itself seemed to lurk in the shadows. But when the flock was under the care of the Good Shepherd, it needn't be afraid. "Your rod and Your staff, they comfort me" (v. 4b). The shepherd was standing guard with his club and his sturdy staff. These were the weapons he had ready in his hands to beat off any animal threatening the flock. His presence, and promised protection, provided "comfort" in what otherwise could be a time of anxiousness and concern.

**WALKING IN OUR LAND**

**OUR TIME IN THE WILDERNESS** is almost over. But what can we carry away from today's visit with David? Let me suggest two abiding truths. First, God is our Good Shepherd, and He has promised to meet our needs—to lead us into pastures of tender grass and to guide us by restful waters. That doesn't mean our lives will be problem-free. This isn't a guarantee of uninterrupted prosperity. But it *is* a promise that God will provide "grace to help in time of need" (Heb. 4:16). Or, as Paul said in Philippians 4:19, "And my God will supply all your needs according to His riches in glory in Christ Jesus." But how can we be sure He'll do this? Because His name—His reputation—is at stake.

Second, as our Good Shepherd God has also promised to protect us from danger. David doesn't say we'll never face danger. There are times when our journey *will* take us through the deep, dark valleys of life. But during those times of trial we can rest assured our God is walking *with* us and watching *over* us. We don't face those threats alone.

Tomorrow we'll continue our study of this amazing psalm. But until then, don't forget that God has promised to be *your* Good Shepherd—if you're one of *His* sheep!

# The Gracious Sovereign

## PSALM 23:5–6

Yesterday we began a two-part study of Psalm 23. The first four verses took us into the Judean Wilderness to view our heavenly Shepherd through the eyes of His earthly flock. Some believe the entire psalm paints a portrait of the Good Shepherd, but I believe David actually captures a different portrait of God in the final two verses. The flocks and wilderness disappear, and the backdrop for this portrait becomes the royal court. The overall message of trust remains the same, but the way David illustrates it changes.

So to get ready for today's journey, put away your hiking boots and walking stick—and slip into something elegant. We're about to enter the banquet hall of the royal palace! Yesterday we saw God as the caring shepherd. But beginning in verse 5 David portrays God as the gracious royal host.

David begins with a bold announcement. "You prepare a table before me in the presence of my enemies" (23:5a). At first, David's word picture seems confusing. For example, if I arrange to buy dinner for you, but the restaurant I pick is in a bad part of town—and filled with criminals, thieves, and cutthroats—you might not be too excited about accepting my invitation! Why would I want to eat in the presence of my enemies?

Some believe David is still using the imagery of a shepherd. They see the "table" as a reference to grass carpeting a hillside—a hillside in plain sight of the predators lurking nearby. And they find support for this idea in Psalm 78:19 where Israel questioned God's provision for them during the exodus by asking, "Can God prepare a table in the wilderness?" Though verse 19 uses the imagery of a table, the psalmist *doesn't* describe God as a shepherd in that part of Psalm 78. Only much later, in verse 52 does he picture God as a shepherd. "He led forth His own people like sheep and guided them in the wilderness like a flock." Could there then be a better interpretation of the final verses in Psalm 23?

While searching for an event in David's life that might explain the imagery, some have seen a parallel to 2 Samuel 17. There, as David was fleeing from Absalom, his friends brought "beds, basins, pottery, wheat, barley, flour, parched grain, beans, lentils, parched seeds, honey, curds, sheep, and cheese of the herd, for David and for the people who were with him, to eat" (17:28–29). They provided necessities for David in a time of need. And yet, other details from that event in David's life just don't seem to fit the picture David paints in Psalm 23.

So what did David have in mind? I believe that beginning in verse 6 David shifts word pictures. He has taken us from the wilderness to the palace. He now pictures himself as a welcomed guest of God. The *table* is the banquet table of his gracious host; God grants bounteous provision for the guest He has chosen to honor. Others who are present might want to harm David, but David is under the protection of his host. He's feasting while they're stewing in their juices because they can't harm someone under the King's protection!

David then announces, "You have anointed my head with oil" (v. 5b). Anointing someone with oil is a concept that is used in several ways in the Bible. In fact, the word "Messiah," *meshiach*, actually refers to someone who was anointed. Kings were anointed, and so were priests. Yet David doesn't use the word *meshiach*. Rather, he uses a Hebrew word that means "to fatten." The particular form David uses communicates the idea of making something fat. He literally says, "You fattened with oil my head,"

An Israeli hotel buffet illustrates the banquet table a king might prepare.

suggesting that the oil was covering his head.

I believe David is continuing his theme of God as the gracious host. From the time of the ancient Egyptians onward olive oil was poured on the heads of guests as an act of courtesy and hospitality. Over a thousand years *after* the time of David the same custom was still being practiced. In Luke 7:46 Jesus drew a comparison between the lack of hospitality shown to Him by His host and the kindness shown to Him by a woman who was a "sinner"—"You did not anoint My head with oil, but she anointed My feet with perfume."

In Psalm 23 David is saying that God, as the ever-gracious host, provided him with protection and showered him with hospitality. In fact, the generosity provided by this gracious heavenly host exceeded all expectations. "My cup overflows" (23:5c). The thought here is that God not only provides what is essential, but He goes far beyond that. Wine was a precious commodity, used and shared sparingly. But God filled David's cup to the brim so that it was ready to spill over.

God's abundance as a gracious King and host was so evident to David that he could come to only one conclusion. "Surely goodness and lovingkindness will follow me all the days of my life, and I will dwell in the house of the LORD forever" (v. 6). The Hebrew word for "goodness" is *tov*, which means "good." This is the same word used in Deuteronomy 28:11, where Moses announced that part of the blessings of the covenant would be that God will "make you abound in *prosperity*" (italics added). Moses then enumerated all the blessings God would pour out on His people.

Paired with God's goodness is God's lovingkindness. The word is *hesed*, which refers to God's loyal, covenant-keeping faithfulness. David was optimistic about the future, but it wasn't based on what David himself could do. Rather, it was oriented toward God's faithfulness to His covenant promises.

David draws his song to a conclusion by saying he would "dwell in the house of the LORD forever." Some believe the "house of the LORD" refers to the Temple, but the temple of Solomon hadn't yet been built. Others think it refers to heaven. But the word "forever" is actually translated from two Hebrew words that mean "length of days." As David pens this psalm he has seen God's gracious blessing thus far in his life, and he is expressing confidence that God will continue to show His loyalty to David through the remainder of David's life. "Eternal life" for a believer does continue on into eternity, but that's not the point David is making here. God *has* been good to David thus far, and David is confident that God's faithfulness will *continue*.

**WALKING IN OUR LAND**

**IT'S TIME TO LEAVE** the banquet hall and begin our journey home. But what truth can we carry along as we head on our way? I'd like to suggest this. We all face threats and problems in our lives regularly, sometimes even daily. At times they can seem almost overwhelming. We can't always choose our circumstances, but we can choose how we're going to respond. David had enemies, but during those times of trouble he also experienced God's loyal love. And remembering how God had worked in the past gave him confidence that God would continue to bless the rest of his life. He rested in the presence of God.

What are your threats today? Take them with you to the royal court of heaven and place them on the banquet table before the King of the universe. Gaze deeply into His loving eyes. And remember: the God who has cared for you in the past is the One who has promised to continue caring for you the rest of your life. If you are one of God's children, you have a *permanent* invitation to dine at His royal banquet table!

# David's Hanukkah Prayer

## PSALM 30

Today's tour takes us into more modern West Jerusalem to visit the Israel Museum and Yad Vashem, Israel's Holocaust Museum. But first we're stopping near the Knesset, Israel's parliament building. Bring your camera and follow me off the bus! I want to show you this beautiful bronze menorah presented to Israel by Britain's Parliament back in 1956.

But while we're here, let me ask you two questions. First, why do some menorahs have seven branches while others have nine? The seven-branched menorahs, like the one near the Knesset, are patterned after the menorah that once stood in the Temple. The nine-branched menorah is for Hanukkah observances. One branch is lit the first night of Hanukkah, and then another is added each night for the eight nights. And the ninth, and center, branch is used to light the other eight branches.

Here's the second question: Did you know that King David wrote a prayer for Hanukkah?

Now, that's something of a trick question, because Hanukkah wasn't established as a festival in Israel until about eight hundred years *after* King David! But one of the psalms used in the celebration of Hanukkah is Psalm 30, and it was written by David! In fact, the opening inscription says David wrote it as a "Song at the Dedication of the House." The Hebrew word for "dedication" is *hanukkah*. The actual Festival of Hanukkah commemorates the rededication of the Temple after it was desecrated by Antiochus Epiphanies. And because of these similarities, it's easy to see why this *hanukkah* prayer of David was later connected with that festival.

The inscription on Psalm 30 has caused problems for some because the original temple wasn't built until *after* the time of David. He wanted to build it, but God didn't allow him to do so. That was left to his son Solomon. So how could David write a psalm for the dedication of the "House" if the Temple didn't exist?

This isn't as serious a problem as it might first seem. The Bible tells us that David gathered all the materials to build the Temple (1 Chron. 22). He purchased the threshing floor of Ornan the Jebusite to be the site where the Temple would ultimately stand (1 Chron. 21:22–25). So David *did* dedicate the land and the materials for the Temple.

But how do Psalm 30, the dedication of the Temple, and Hanukkah relate to us today? I'm glad you asked! To answer that question, let's journey back to when David was gathering materials for Solomon's temple. It was a time of national prosperity and peace. Unfortunately, it was also a time when David's pride nearly destroyed his kingdom!

The events of 1 Chronicles 21 are almost certainly the background for David's prayer in Psalm 30. First

Bronze Menorah that stands near the entrance to the Knesset, Israel's parliament building.

Chronicles 21 begins with David making a foolish decision to order a census of all the men of Israel who could serve in his army (vv. 1–5). He wasn't facing any danger at the time. His purpose was just to satisfy his own pride. "Look how great I've become! Look at the army I can field!" And indeed it was impressive. He had the potential to field an army more than a million strong.

God responded to David's pride by sending a plague through the land that reached all the way to Jerusalem. David repented, humbling himself before God. He purchased the land where the Temple would later sit and offered sacrifices to the Lord. The account in Chronicles ends with David issuing a command: "The house of the LORD God is to be here" (1 Chron. 22:1 NIV).

A prideful sense of security, followed by God's chastening, followed by a personal recognition of wrong and a humble submission to God. These historical events are the themes David actually develops in the prayer of Psalm 30.

David begins his prayer by praising God for His deliverance. "I will extol You, O LORD, for You have lifted me up, and have not let my enemies rejoice over me" (30:1). When David saw the angel of the Lord poised above Jerusalem, sword in hand, he understood how tenuous his life really was. Now, as he reflects back on those events, he realizes God had taken him to the edge of death itself and then brought him back. "O LORD, You have brought up my soul from Sheol; You have kept me alive, that I would not go down to the pit" (v. 3).

David pauses in his prayer to remind his audience of a lesson they can learn from his recent experience. "Sing praises to the LORD, you His godly ones, and give thanks to His holy name. For His anger is but for a moment, His favor is for a lifetime; weeping may last for the night, but a shout of joy comes in the morning" (30:4–5).

There *are* times when God needs to discipline us as His children. There *are* consequences for our foolish, sinful decisions and actions. But David wanted others to realize that those times of discipline are only temporary for those who are truly God's children. Times of correction, painful though they may be, are followed by our heavenly Father's loving embrace.

Returning to his prayer, David confesses the pride that led him to act so foolishly. "I said in my prosperity, 'I will never be moved,'" (v. 6). David looked at all he had and felt invincible, unmovable. After all, he had a million-man army! But that's when the unthinkable happened. God "hid [His] face" in judgment, and David suddenly felt "dismayed" (v. 7). He continues his prayer to God. "To you, O LORD, I called, and to the Lord I made supplication . . . Hear, O Lᴏʀᴅ, and be gracious to me; O Lᴏʀᴅ, be my helper" (vv. 8, 10).

In 1 Chronicles 21:16 David repented of his pride by clothing himself in sackcloth, demonstrating his humble submission to God. And he ends his prayer in Psalm 30 by focusing again on what God had done. "You have turned for me my mourning into dancing; You have loosed my sackcloth and girded me with gladness" (30:11). God *did* respond to David in his time of distress!

**WALKING IN OUR LAND**

**WE CAN LEARN** two lessons from David's prayer in Psalm 30. First, the prayer of the shepherd boy turned king is a reminder of the truth that God is "opposed to the proud, but gives grace to the humble" (James 4:6; 1 Peter 5:5). It was David's pride that brought him low . . . and God's grace that restored him once he humbled himself. Voices all around you are telling you to demand your rights and to boast in your achievements. But Psalm 30 is a reminder that followers of Jesus are to follow a different path, one in which selfish pride is replaced with humble submission. We're not the masters of our fate or the captains of our souls.[1] He is! And we need to tell Him that!

Second, God *does* respond to the humble prayers of His children. If you're struggling with the consequences of poor choices and foolish actions in the past, just remember, it's never too late to return to God. He specializes in restoring those who have strayed. Or, as David wrote so poetically in this psalm: "For his anger lasts only a moment, but his favor lasts a lifetime; weeping may remain for a night, but rejoicing comes in the morning" (30:5 NIV).

And that's another great reason to pray!

# Where Is God When It Hurts?

## PSALMS 42–43

As Job sat on the ash heap in agony, three "friends" came by to offer comfort. Mixing flawed observations on life with bad theology, they thought Job's suffering was God's punishment for sin, and they concluded that Job was unrighteous.

Job knew he was innocent of their charges. But since he didn't know why he was suffering, he decided God was unfair. Only the readers of the book know the true story: Job's condition was part of a larger cosmic struggle between God and Satan.

We all face times of tremendous struggle and doubt, times when we have many questions but few answers. A lost job. A house in danger of foreclosure. Physical or emotional trauma. Sudden, often unexpected, loss of a loved one. Tragic events that tear through lives, leaving in their wake broken dreams, unfulfilled hopes, and crushed spirits. During such times of struggle the often unspoken question is simply this: "Where is God when it hurts?"

The writer of Psalms 42 and 43 knew the sting of personal pain. These two psalms were intended to be read as a single composition with three separate stanzas. Each stanza ends with virtually the same refrain: "Why are you in despair, O my soul? And why are you disturbed within me? Hope in God, for I shall again praise Him, the help of my countenance and my God" (43:5; see also 42:5, 11).

In the first stanza (42:1–5), the psalmist looked fondly to the past even as he lamented his present condition. He thirsted for God much as a deer thirsts for water in times of drought. Tearfully he contrasted the present jeers of his captors ("Where is your God?") to the past joy he had experienced when he journeyed to Jerusalem to worship the Lord.

In the second stanza (42:6–11), the psalmist rehearsed the pain and confusion he felt at being carried into exile from the land of Israel. The progression he gives is from "the land of the Jordan" (the Jordan Valley) to "the peaks of Hermon" (in northern Israel) to "Mount Mizar" (one of the lower peaks of Mount Hermon). While his desire was to travel south *toward* God's temple in Jerusalem, he

The Banias Waterfall near Mount Hermon.

was being carried *north* into captivity, away from the very land God had promised His people.

The psalmist pictured his turmoil, pain, confusion, and heartache as if their crushing weight were a roaring waterfall relentlessly pounding down on him. Perhaps he had just walked very near the Banias Waterfall that today thunders at the base of Mount Hermon. The deep roar of that cascading water can be heard even before the waterfall is in sight. When I take a group to the Banias Waterfall, they look up at the majestic water crashing on to the rocks below and see incredible beauty. But to the psalmist, those same waters illustrated the terrible weight of sorrow that seemed to overwhelm him. In his pain he cried out to God in verse 9, "Why have You forgotten me?"

The psalmist's answer to his own penetrating question comes in two parts. The first is a remarkable reminder of God's faithfulness. "The LORD will command His lovingkindness in the daytime; and His song will be with me in the night, a prayer to the God of my life" (42:8). This is the only time in these two psalms where the psalmist refers to God as the "LORD" (using the Hebrew word *Yahweh* to refer to the covenant-keeping God). Though the writer may *feel* abandoned and alone, God is still present—and still working on behalf of His people. God's loyal love and words of comfort are active day and night, even when our circumstances might make us feel otherwise.

The second answer to one of life's hardest questions comes in the final stanza of this three-stanza psalm (43:1–5). The psalmist gained perspective and hope by going to God in prayer and by focusing on the future. His problems seemed overwhelming, but he needed to remember that God's power is greater than any possible difficulty he might be facing. As a result, he could ask God to rescue him and to guide him through life's flood-waters. The psalmist ended with a sense of expectancy and hope. He knew that someday he would make his way back to Jerusalem to worship God. He didn't know how everything would work out, but he was convinced God would answer his heartfelt prayer. And this gave him renewed hope.

## WALKING IN OUR LAND

**PERHAPS THREE MILLENNIA** ago the sons of Korah wrote these two psalms. Placing our hope in God is an approach many have accepted since then. Among the images of trust in our Creator's good plans that at times we cannot see is that of a beautifully woven tapestry, which from the back-side looks chaotic and totally unappealing. An anonymous poem titled "The Weaver," first appeared in the late nineteenth century.[1] The poem affirms many of the lessons of Psalms 42–43.

### THE WEAVER

My life is but a weaving
Between my Lord and me,
I cannot choose the colors
He worketh steadily.

Oftimes He weaveth sorrow,
And I in foolish pride
Forget He sees the upper
And I, the under side.

Not till the loom is silent
And the shuttles cease to fly
Shall God unroll the canvas
And explain the reason why.

The dark threads are as needful
In the Weaver's skillful hand
As the threads of gold and silver
In the pattern He has planned.

Are you feeling overwhelmed by your problems? Does God seem strangely silent and distant? Go to Him in prayer, and let Him know how you feel. Don't be afraid to share your hurts and disappointments. But then step back and realize that your problems may be obscuring your view of God. Remember, God is still with you, even if you don't sense His presence. And like the confusing backside of a tapestry still being woven, you are being woven by God into a beautiful work, a work still in progress.

Memorize Psalm 42:8 to remind yourself that God will stay beside you all day and through the night. Yesterday might hold bitter memories, and today may bring troubles cascading down on you, threatening to sweep you away. But look to God for tomorrow, gain His eternal perspective, and watch Him turn your heartache into hope.

Those words from Korah's sons remain true today, and worthy of our prayer: "Why are you in despair, O my soul? And why are you disturbed within me? Hope in God, for I shall again praise Him, the help of my countenance and my God" (43:5).

# The City of Our God

## PSALM 46

Have you ever noticed how many restaurant chains claim to have a special ingredient that makes their food unique? KFC has its "*secret blend* of eleven herbs and spices," while McDonald's Big Mac is made with "two all-beef patties, *special sauce*, lettuce, cheese, pickles, onion, on a sesame-seed bun!" These unidentified ingredients are that "special something" that supposedly sets the food apart and gives it that irresistible taste.

Cities often have something unique that also makes them special. Would London, Paris, or New York be the same without Big Ben, the Eiffel Tower, or the Empire State Building and Statue of Liberty? In fact, most world-class cities seem to have something iconic that embodies their character and essence. Jerusalem is no exception, though its "secret sauce" might just surprise you. It's not a physical structure, like the Dome of the

Rock or the walls of the Old City.

No, the secret sauce that makes Jerusalem so special is the God who chose the city as His own. As the writer of Psalm 46 says, Jerusalem is "the city of God" and "God is in the midst of her" (46:4–5).

Psalm 46 is a psalm of fearless trust in the God who demonstrates His power and love. Martin Luther based his hymn, *Ein feste Burg ist unser Gott* ("A Mighty Fortress Is Our God") on Psalm 46, and the power and majesty of this psalm *are* captured in the words and melody of that hymn.

The psalm itself seems to divide into three sections, each of which ends with the Hebrew word *Selah*. That word is used seventy-four times in the Old Testament,

The temple complex depicted in the model of the Second Temple, Jerusalem.

with seventy-one of those appearing in the book of Psalms. Though not everyone agrees on its meaning, the word seems to indicate a break or pause in the text. The Amplified Bible might have captured the essential understanding of the word when it translated *selah* as "pause, and calmly think of that."

The psalm begins by boldly stating its theme. "God is our refuge and strength, a very present help in trouble." The writer then paints two very dramatic pictures of the kind of trouble we can face. In verses 2–3 he says we can trust God even if *nature* seems to turn upside down, while in verses 5–7 he says we can trust God even if *nations* seem to turn upside down.

In his first word picture the psalmist describes the very undoing of creation. At the time of creation God brought dry land out of the sea, but the psalmist pictures a time of chaos when even the mountains will once again "slip into the heart of the sea" (v. 2). A time might come when that which we thought was rock-solid, stable, and secure—like the mountains—could become like Jell-O and melt into the raging, foamy deep. But even if the unthinkable were to happen, the psalmist says "we will not fear" because God is greater than any force of nature.

In his second picture the psalmist turns from nature to nations. Instead of the chaos of the raging sea, the writer describes the uproar among the nations as kingdoms totter. The people are now threatened not by natural disaster but by the threats of sinister, evil empires intent on Jerusalem's destruction. The danger is real—but so is the God who watches over His city. The people are able to shout in triumph, "The LORD of hosts is with us; the God of Jacob is our stronghold" (v. 7). The phrase "LORD of hosts" is *Yahweh Tzebaot*, God of the heavenly forces. Neither nature nor nations are any match for the heavenly hosts under God's control!

Well, this might all be well and good, but what does all this have to do with Jerusalem's "secret sauce"? Well I'm glad you asked! Because in the midst of describing all the threats from nature and nations, the writer pauses to focus on Jerusalem, the city that is ground zero in the conflict. At first, his description of Jerusalem seems both inaccurate and inappropriate. "There is a river whose streams make glad the city of God, the holy dwelling places of the Most High" (v. 4).

If you visit Jerusalem, one thing you will *not* see is a river! Egypt has the Nile, Babylon the Euphrates, and Nineveh the Tigris. But there is no physical river in Jerusalem, and that's the key to let us know the writer has something else in mind. The "river" providing life to Jerusalem was the sustaining, nurturing power of God

Almighty. That's why the psalmist calls Jerusalem "the city of God." It was God's presence in the city that provided all that it needed. In the very next verse he makes this clear. "God is in the midst of her, she will not be moved; God will help her when morning dawns" (46:5).

## WALKING IN OUR LAND

**NATURE AND NATIONS.** Both were threats to Jerusalem. And both remain threats to us today. God wanted Jerusalem to realize that His presence and His power were sufficient for their protection. In fact, as the psalm draws to a close, God Himself speaks to the people. "Cease striving and know that I am God; I will be exalted among the nations, I will be exalted in the earth" (v. 10). God is greater than both nations and nature. He's powerful enough to handle any threat. And that's why our job is to "cease striving," which literally means "let it drop" in the sense of letting your arms relax and drop to your side. Stop trying to fight the battles in your own power . . . and come to know, experientially, that the One in your midst really is God!

The psalm ends with the people acknowledging what God has just said. They triumphantly affirm, "The LORD of hosts is with us; the God of Jacob is our stronghold" (46:11). Is your world dissolving around you? Are you facing problems that seem to be coming at you from all directions? Pause and remember that God is in your midst. And at His command are all the forces of heaven itself. Let your weary arms drop to your side, and allow Him to fight your spiritual battles. You'll find His grace and strength to be sufficient.

Appropriately enough, the psalm ends with that word *Selah*, or as the Amplified Bible translated it: "pause, and calmly think of that."

# The Battle That Never Was

## Psalm 48

The greatest way to get to know Jerusalem is on foot. Granted, it's also the slowest and most strenuous. But walking along its ramparts, hiking around its walls, and wandering through its streets and alleys comprise the single best way to understand the city. There is no substitute for having your feet pound the pavement to get a feel for this amazing city.

Today you'll have an opportunity to do just that. We're going to join the sons of Korah on a walking tour around the walls of Jerusalem! So grab your hat and knapsack and join us to celebrate the battle that never was, as we look at Psalm 48.

This psalm of celebration begins by focusing our attention on God. "Great is the Lord and greatly to be praised" (v. 1). We can praise God for *who* He is or for *what* He has done. And this psalm calls on us to praise

God for what He's done for the city of Jerusalem, but the psalmist takes us on a roundabout journey to make his point.

The first several verses employ a literary style we call a *chiasm*. It's a Semitic way of thinking and writing where the psalmist begins and ends a section by saying essentially the same thing. For example, he begins verse 1 by telling us that God is worthy of praise, and he ends this first section in verse 3 by telling us *why* God is worthy of such praise. "God, in her palaces, has made Himself known as a stronghold."

Having told us why we need to praise our God, the writer then explains *where* the people ought to praise Him. He says in verse 1 that it should happen "in the city of our God." He restates the location at the end of verse 2. We're to offer this praise in "the city of the great King." Because the word "King" is parallel to "our God," we know the psalmist isn't talking about the human ruler of Jerusalem. The king we're to praise is the sovereign King of the universe!

Finally, in the very center of this first section the psalmist leads us to the Temple. That's where he wants us to gather to praise God. The procession is heading toward "His holy mountain," which the psalmist then identifies as "Mount Zion in the far north." Evidently this psalm was written to commemorate a national gathering of the people at Solomon's temple on the north side of Jerusalem.

But, you might ask yourself, why are we gathering at the Temple today to praise God? The writer shares the answer in verses 4–7. We're gathered to thank God for saving us from our enemies. Kings had "assembled themselves" to attack Jerusalem. The psalmist doesn't identify the kings or the battle, but it seems likely that the attack he has in mind is the invasion by King Sennacherib of Assyria in 701 BC. That year Sennacherib led his army against King Hezekiah of Jerusalem (see 2 Kings 18:13,

Walls of the old city of Jerusalem outside the Citadel of David.

19–25; 19:1–4), and it looked as if Jerusalem would surely fall. But something very dramatic happened that changed the course of the battle.

Anyone who has studied Latin has likely read Julius Caesar's staccato account to the Roman Senate of his swift victory in battle. "*Veni. Vidi. Vici.*" Translated, that's "I came. I saw. I conquered." Using similar verbs the writer of Psalm 48 pictures the menacing attack of Assyria's mighty army—but with a surprising twist. They "passed by together." They "saw." But then, they "fled in alarm." Maybe we would translate it into Latin as "*Veni. Vidi. Vegematic.*" "They came. They saw. They got chopped to pieces!"

The mighty army of Assyria arrived at Jerusalem. But rather than conquering the city, the psalmist says they were "terrified" and "fled in alarm" (v. 5). He pictures the destruction like a powerful storm shattering and sinking a helpless ship caught out on the open ocean. "With the east wind You break the ships of Tarshish" (v. 7).

In verse 8 the writer shares the key lesson he wants the people to know and remember: "As we have heard, so have we seen." They had heard about God's miracles in the past. They knew about the crossing of the Red Sea and the drowning of Pharaoh's army. But *now* they had seen God's power in action with their own eyes. God had again miraculously intervened to deliver His people!

Leaving the Temple, the psalmist encouraged the worshipers to take a walking tour of the city's defenses. "Walk about Zion and go around her; count her towers; consider her ramparts; go through her palaces" (vv. 12–13). But what is it he wants us to see on this tour? Well, let's go have a look!

Examine carefully the city's walls. Not a single stone has been shattered by an Assyrian battering ram. No dirt is piled against the walls to mark the spot where a siege ramp was constructed. In fact, there's not a single spot anywhere around the city to even hint at the fact that the Assyrians were planning to attack—and then the point being made by the psalmist hits you. The walls were untouched because *God* defeated Jerusalem's enemies before they could even begin attacking the city. The physical walls hadn't really been Jerusalem's protection at all. It was God who had protected the city in response to the people's prayers.

The psalmist smiles, and then he drives home this point in his final verse. "For such is God, our God forever and ever; He will guide us until death."

**WALKING IN OUR LAND**

**SO WHAT ARE** the forces threatening your life right now? It might be physical or financial foes threatening to destroy your security. It could be emotional or spiritual enemies, and you worry that you won't be strong enough to hold them off.

Take time to read the account of the Assyrian attack on Jerusalem in Isaiah 36–37. Then reread Psalm 48. The people of Jerusalem had heard of God's miracles in the past. But now they saw for themselves what God could do—up close and personal—in their own hour of need. Psalm 48 was written to remind *future* generations, including you, that we can *still* depend on God to be a very present help in time of need.

Just like King Hezekiah and the people of Jerusalem, take your problems to God and lay them out before Him in prayer. Then watch as He works in His own special way to meet *your* need. Because, as the psalmist said in verse 14, "such is God, our God forever and ever; He will guide us until death."

# Tears in a Bottle

## PSALM 56

Watch your step! This roadway down the Mount of Olives is very steep, and I don't want anybody to slip and fall on some loose gravel. You made it past the hoard of peddlers selling all their trinkets, and now it's just a little less hectic. But that's only for a short while. See that opening to the right about fifty feet ahead? It's the entrance to Dominus Flevit, our next stop!

There's so much we can talk about at this site. The ossuaries, or bone boxes, near the entrance. The beautiful view of Jerusalem from inside. Or the thorn trees in front of the chapel that so vividly picture what the crown of thorns might have been like. But today I want to point out one unusual architectural feature of the chapel itself. Look carefully at its four corners. See those decorative urns rising up on each side? Those actually represent tear bottles. This chapel commemorates the place where Jesus wept over Jerusalem—Dominus Flevit means "our Lord wept"—so the architect incorporated tear bottles into his design.

But why tear bottles? What's the story behind them?

Excavators have found numerous small, blown-glass bottles from New Testament times that were used to collect someone's tears. It was as if, by collecting their tears in a bottle, people could hang on to the memories of their loved ones through times of separation and loss. It was a tangible way to demonstrate how much you cared for somebody. The architect placed these bottles on each corner to honor the tears Jesus shed for this city and its people.

Tear bottles decorate the corners on the *Dominus Flevit* chapel on the Mount of Olives.

Take one final look at those bottles, because I want to transport us to a different time and a different place. And the only similarity to what we've seen so far will be those tear bottles. Our destination is the city of Gath out on the Philistine Plain, and our arrival time is a thousand years *before* the time of Jesus. We've arrived in a city controlled by the Philistines who are at war with Israel, their sworn enemies.

We're in enemy territory. And what's more, so is young David! In his desperate attempt to flee from King Saul, David foolishly thought he would be safe by fleeing to this Philistine city. But the Philistine leaders had a sharp eye, and an even sharper memory. The battle in the Elah Valley had been short and chaotic, but they recognized the young shepherd lad who had killed the champion of Gath, the giant Goliath! The leaders confronted the king with their accusation. "Is this not David the king of the land? Did they not sing of this one as they danced, saying, 'Saul has slain his thousands, and David his ten thousands'?" (1 Sam. 21:11).

When David heard these words, his heart sank. In fleeing from Saul to the city of Gath, David had jumped out of the frying pan and right into the fire. For one of the few times in his life the Bible says David "greatly feared" his enemies (v. 12). In desperation young David feigned insanity, hoping to convince the king he was no longer a threat. And surprisingly the king of Gath did allow him to leave. David was still a fugitive from Saul, but at least he was no longer trapped inside this enemy stronghold.

But what does David's near-death experience in Gath have to do with tear bottles? The answer comes from the very psalm written by David after his heart-pounding escape from this Philistine city. In the introduction to Psalm 56, David tells us he wrote the psalm "when the Philistines seized him in Gath." This psalm is a poetic retelling of his life-threatening experience in that stronghold.

David begins his psalm with a description of being trampled on and oppressed by his enemies. No doubt the nobles who seized him and took him before the king wanted permission to exact their revenge on this one who had killed their champion and defeated their armies. David had good reason to be afraid. The threat to his life was real.

But David then shared the inner thought process that made him such a man after God's own heart. Listen carefully to what he wrote in verses 3 and 4. "When I am afraid, I will put my trust in You. In God, whose word I praise, in God I have put my trust; I shall not be afraid. What can mere man do to me?" In his darkest hour David understood the power of the God in whom he trusted was greater than that of the enemies aligned against him.

This is, of course, a noble thought! But some of you might be thinking, *I know God is greater than all the problems I face. But how can I be sure He cares enough for me to help? He might be great, but is He also good?*

Just a few verses later David shares his reassuring answer to this provocative question. With confidence he cries out in verse 8, "You have taken account of my wanderings; put my tears in Your bottle. Are they not in Your book?"

A bottle and a book. David uses these two objects to describe how much God cares for His children. As David wept in fear and anguish, he pictured God gently pressing His heavenly tear bottle against David's cheek, carefully collecting each tear falling from his eyes. God wasn't listening passively to David's cries for help; He was lovingly saving up David's tears. This psalm paints a tender picture of David's preciousness to God. And, by extension, David demonstrates the preciousness in which God holds *all* His children.

David's second example shifts our focus from a tear bottle to a book. His struggles and problems were, he said, recorded in God's heavenly book. The truth being conveyed is that God knows *everything* that's taking place in our lives. Nothing escapes His notice, nothing is missed. David has confidence in God because he knows God is aware of every moment and every circumstance . . . and He won't forget them.

Tear bottles. They commemorate a time when the Son of God wept over Jerusalem. In Psalm 56 they also remind us that God cares for His followers, especially in times of anguish. David's message for his readers is simple. If you're struggling today, God knows, and He cares! This leads David to shout triumphantly in the very next verse, "This I know, that God is for me" (v. 9).

**WALKING IN OUR LAND**

**SO WHAT PROBLEMS** are you facing today? What anxieties are keeping you up at night? What sorrows are staining your cheeks with tears? Realize this. God saves up and cherishes your tears. He records all your experiences in His heavenly diary to make sure nothing is ever forgotten.

Whatever you're facing today, you *can* trust in God to watch over you. He knows . . . and He cares.

# The Grateful Pilgrim

## PSALM 84

Talk with individuals who have traveled to the Holy Land and you will probably hear some recurring themes. "The trip made the Bible come alive." "I felt like I was home." "I sensed a closeness to God." "It helped me grow spiritually."

Those who have visited Israel struggle when they return to put their thoughts and emotions into words. The trip makes a profound spiritual impact that most find hard to describe. Perhaps that's why God placed Psalm 84 into Israel's inspired songbook. This is the song of the grateful pilgrim, a song that seeks to put into words the spiritual impact of such a visit. So let's sit down with the anonymous writer to hear his "Holy Land experience."

We don't know where the psalmist was from, though we can assume he lived somewhere in the land of Israel. But we definitely know where he wanted to go. He had

Hiking trail in the Banias Nature Reserve.

his heart set on visiting the Temple in Jerusalem! Perhaps he was traveling there for one of the three annual pilgrimages. But whatever the specific reason, his soul "longed and even yearned for the courts of LORD" (Ps. 84:2).

But what is it about this trip that has so profoundly impacted our pilgrim? Well, he instinctively knows the journey is connected in a special way to the God he loves. It's not just the beautiful temple buildings that draws him to Jerusalem. In fact, he doesn't even describe it as the "house" of God. Instead, the word he uses is the word for "tent" or "tabernacle." It's not the buildings themselves, but the God who dwells in them that makes the journey so special.

The writer searches for ways to describe his intense desire to visit this place so closely connected to God. He thinks about those who are privileged to spend time at the Temple. From the tiniest of "swallows" nesting high in the courtyard rafters to the priests ministering at the altars, "How blessed are those who dwell in Your house!" (v. 4).

Beginning in verse 5 the psalmist focuses on the blessings reserved for the pilgrim "in whose heart are the highways to Zion." The highways he has in mind are those that lead toward God's temple in Jerusalem. And it's here where the writer provides his most vivid illustration of the impact the trip has on a pilgrim's life. Yet sadly, most of us miss what he's saying. So let's slow down and look carefully at his description of the journey.

"Passing through the valley of Baca they make it a spring" (v. 6). But where's the valley of Baca, and how can pilgrims turn it into a spring? There is no specific valley in the Bible or in the Holy Land named Baca. Used as a noun, the word *baca* referred to the balsam tree, the tree that produced the "balm of Gilead" mentioned in the Bible. The balsam tree would "weep," or "drip," a resinous gum that was collected and used to produce the healing balm. As a result, when the word *baca* is used as a verb, it means to weep, wail, or lament.

Rather than identifying a specific physical location, the psalmist probably is describing the *emotional impact* of his pilgrimage. The journey to Jerusalem took his sadness and sorrow, represented by the "valley of Baca," and replaced it with a "spring." Water here is a symbol of life, abundance, and ultimately joy. Lest we miss the point, he immediately adds that "the early rain also covers it with blessing." The "early rain" was part of the blessing promised by God to Israel in Deuteronomy 11. God is showering His blessings on the pilgrim as he makes his way toward God's house in Jerusalem.

The journey to Jerusalem was physically exhausting.

It was a grueling trek for the Old Testament pilgrims, and in some ways it still is for travelers today. But rather than growing weary on the journey, the pilgrim would "go from strength to strength" (v. 7). This traveler discovered an unknown, unexplained sustaining power that kept him strong as he journeyed to appear before God in Zion.

The journey also had a *spiritual impact* on the pilgrim, and the psalmist ends with a prayer to God (vv. 8–12), whom he first addresses as "the Lord God of hosts" (v. 8) or the God of the mighty armies of heaven. While he asks God to protect the king, whom he describes as Israel's "shield" and as God's "anointed" (v. 9), he later acknowledges that ultimately God is Israel's "sun and shield" (v. 11). The journey has reaffirmed the pilgrim's trust in his God.

How significant is the impact of this journey on the pilgrim? "A day in Your courts is better than a thousand outside" (v. 10). I often tell people that a two-week trip to Israel is the equivalent of spending a year in Bible college or seminary, but it turns out I've been underselling it! As the psalmist describes it, a *single day* is worth "a thousand" anywhere else.

But how can that be true? The psalmist seems to provide an answer as he draws his song to a close. I actually like the King James translation of the next phrase in verse 10. "I had rather be a doorkeeper in the house of my God, than to dwell in the tents of wickedness." The most humble position serving God in Jerusalem was far more desirable than time spent living in "tents of wickedness," or places of unrestrained self-gratification. What happens in Vegas might stay in Vegas, but what happens to a person in Israel impacts that person forever! This is true because the God we encounter during our pilgrimage is a God who "gives grace and glory" and a God who doesn't withhold any "good thing . . . from those who walk uprightly" (v. 11).

**WALKING IN OUR LAND**

**AS WE TURN TO LEAVE,** let's think back over the lessons our special pilgrimage has shared. A journey to the Holy Land provides new insight into the God we love, and helps us understand life more clearly from His perspective. We might start our journey carrying a heavy load of care and pain, but along the way God somehow replaces our feelings of sorrow with tears of joy. He provides physical strength and spiritual blessing.

During the journey we come to understand what is truly significant, valuable, and lasting in life. When we began, we knew God was omnipotent, but we have discovered He is *our* shield. We knew He was omnipresent, but we have come to realize He has chosen to work in a special way in this unique part of the world. We knew He was omniscient, but we found ourselves looking on His face and learning more about Him as we walked through the land where He revealed so much about Himself. God didn't change during our journey, but He *did* change us. As a result, we will *never* be the same again!

# A Song from the Wilderness

## PSALM 90

I'll never forget our three-day journey through the wilderness during my first trip to Israel, completed at the end of the second week of a three-week study tour. The entire group was physically exhausted and emotionally weary. Late on a Sunday afternoon we finally drove into the town of Arad, perched on the edge of the Judean Wilderness.

The previous day one of the faculty members on the trip had received a phone call telling him his adult daughter had passed away. Her death wasn't unexpected because she had been fighting a losing battle with cancer. But the bleakness of our surroundings matched the heartache and loss we all felt on behalf of this professor and his family.

Before checking into the hotel for the night, we stopped outside town for an informal worship service.

Wayne, the professor whose daughter had died, was scheduled to speak. We asked if he wanted someone else to fill in, but he felt God wanted him to share what was on his heart.

I'm so glad he did, because what he shared was one of the most powerful messages I have ever heard, made even more so by the location and circumstances in which it was given.

As we sat on the ground and opened our Bibles, the sun was descending toward the horizon. A thousand shadows slipped out of their daytime hiding places, and the interplay of light and darkness highlighted every twisting hill and valley in the wilderness before us. The hills took on a soft glow of gold and tan that signaled the approach of evening. A cool breeze blew across our backs, drying our sweat and bringing with it a slight chill.

With the wilderness as his backdrop, Wayne opened his Bible to Psalm 90, the oldest of the psalms. Psalm 90 is a psalm penned by Israel's first great leader, a psalm intended to be sung, as it were, in a minor key.

As Wayne read the psalm aloud, I gazed out over the barren hills and pictured Moses sitting, pen in hand, outside his tent in a wilderness very similar to that in front of me. Perhaps he could hear the soft wail of a family in the distance returning to camp after burying yet another loved one. Moses was leading a nation locked in a holding pattern, waiting for an entire generation to perish before God would let them move forward.

You can almost smell the dust from the desert in every verse of Psalm 90. The psalm contains the somber reflections of a leader condemned to watch an entire generation die for its disobedience. As it begins, Moses probably is looking out at the stark, unchanging landscape that reminded him of the eternality of God. "Before the mountains were born or You gave birth to the earth and the world, even from everlasting to everlasting, You are God" (v. 2).

Looking out into the wilderness.

Moses begins by focusing on the fact that God is eternal, but in verses 3–6 he notes sadly that God's creation is not. And in these verses Moses turns to gaze on the people around him. Humanity was the climax of God's creation, but humans were still finite beings who, Moses solemnly records, are destined to return "back to dust" (v. 3), just as God had said to Adam.

In these verses, Moses likens death's unexpected arrival to a deadly winter storm sending a wall of water rushing down a desert canyon, sweeping away everything in its path. In that same sudden, unexpected way God would "sweep people away in the sleep of death" (v. 5 NIV). Or, comparing the brevity of life to grass that "in the morning . . . sprouts anew" during the winter rains, Moses saw an entire lifespan as if it sprang up in the morning, only to be gone by evening.

God is eternal, but we're not. Having penned the book of Genesis, Moses knew that death was the result of God's judgment on human sin and disobedience—from the disobedience of Adam to the sins of the children of Israel in the wilderness. And in verses 7–10, Moses reminds his readers of this fact. Death *is* God's judgment for sin. "You have placed our iniquities before You, our secret sins in the light of Your presence" (v. 8).

How long are we here on earth? Moses supplies the

answer in verse 10. "Our days may come to seventy years, or eighty, if our strength endures; yet the best of them are but trouble and sorrow, for they quickly pass, and we fly away" (NIV). Life is short. Time flies by, and we finish "our years like a sigh" (v. 9). Life is indeed as fleeting—and often, it seems, as sad—as a mournful sigh.

As noted earlier, this psalm was supposed to be sung in a minor key. But it was not intended to be a cynical reflection on life's futility. No indeed! Moses took a clear-eyed look at life to help us understand its real essence. He broke down human existence into its essential components—life, death, and the God of eternity.

Verse 12 is the turning point for the psalm. "Teach us to number our days, that we may present to You a heart of wisdom." Understanding life's brevity helps us realize the importance of God's eternal wisdom. We need to acquire His perspective on what is truly important, His perspective on what is truly valuable, and His perspective on what is truly eternal.

Moses concludes his psalm with three lessons from the wilderness that can help us gain that heart of wisdom. First, in verses 14–15 Moses reminds us of our need to seek after God and His *mercy*. "Satisfy us in the morning with Your lovingkindness, that we may sing for joy and be glad all our days." Every morning in the wilderness Israel experienced a visible reminder of God's unfailing love—the manna. For forty years they had an object lesson of what Jesus told us to pray for in Matthew: "Give us this day our daily bread" (6:11). Moses is telling us we can find joy in life by watching for God's acts of compassion and unfailing love, even in the midst of life's difficulties.

Second, in verse 16 Moses reminds his listeners to focus on God's *majesty*. "Let Your work appear to Your servants, and Your majesty to their children." The wilderness was a place of hardship and testing, but the wilderness was also a place where the faithful discovered a God of splendor who answers prayer and meets needs—from the cloud by day and the pillar of fire by night for guidance to the food and water needed to sustain life and protection from their enemies. When our need is great, that's when we discover His surpassing grace is even greater.

Finally, Moses encourages the people to remember God's *ministry*. He ends his poem by repeating the same request twice. "Confirm for us the work of our hands; yes, confirm the work of our hands" (v. 17). Most people want to do something to give meaning to their life. They strive for significance, for something that extends beyond their brief time here on earth. But such efforts are futile unless God gives those labors eternal value.

**WALKING IN OUR LAND**

**WHAT DOES IT TAKE** to transform casual Christians into passionate followers of Christ whose lives make an eternal impact on their world? Ultimately, it's the truth found in Psalm 90. The life we live here on earth is fleeting and ends in death. God wants us to live this life with our eyes focused on Him—and on the life to come.

British missionary C. T. Studd captured the essence of Psalm 90 in a poem he wrote titled "Only One Life." The poem begins with these words:

> Two little lines I heard one day,
> Traveling along life's busy way;
> Bringing conviction to my heart,
> And from my mind would not depart;
> Only one life, 'twill soon be past,
> Only what's done for Christ will last.[1]

# Under His Wings

## PSALM 91

I'm often asked if I've ever been afraid while traveling in Israel, and my answer is, "Not really!" It's amazing how safe I've felt all the times I've been there.

Well, there was the time when our driver took a wrong turn, and we ended up in a village where we really shouldn't have gone. But nothing happened. I also remember feeling ill at ease once while walking through the old city of Jerusalem late at night. But again, it turned out that there really wasn't anything to be afraid of.

The only time I *was* genuinely concerned happened on a hike through the very wilderness shown on the next pages of this chapter. It was during a student trip on a hot summer day. The sun was relentless, the hike was hard, and I'd already used up the water in both of my canteens. I remember how exhausted I felt and how much I really wanted just two things—something cold to drink and a shady spot to rest! For about an hour my life boiled down to those two essentials!

If you have ever experienced physical exhaustion and extreme thirst, then you can appreciate Psalm 91, a psalm that focuses on the security God provides to those who trust in Him. To help you understand the psalm, let's look at the big picture first, and then we'll look at the specifics in more detail.

The psalm can be divided into two or three sections, and each of those divisions can be helpful. When we divide it into two eight-verse segments, we can see some

Late afternoon shadows appear on the vast, arid Judean Wilderness.

amazing parallels. Each section begins with two verses of assurance, promising security to those who take refuge in God. And in both sections the psalmist promises God's protection from two very specific enemies.

But the psalm can also be divided into three sections based on the subject. In verses 1 and 2 the psalmist talks about himself: "I will say." Then in verses 3 through 13 he focuses on the audience: "He who delivers you. . . . He will cover you. . . . You will not be afraid" (vv. 3–5). In the final three verses the one doing the speaking is God: "Because he has loved Me, therefore I will deliver him" (v. 14a).

With either division of Psalm 91, the focus is on God's security for those who trust in Him. The one "who dwells in the shelter of the Most High will abide in the shadow of the Almighty" (v. 1). Those who go to God for refuge will find the shelter and protection they seek. In verse 2 the psalmist affirms his own personal trust in God. God is "my refuge and my fortress, my God, in whom I trust!" The word he uses for fortress is *metsudah*, Masada, the name later given to Herod the Great's desert fortress by the Dead Sea (recall our visit to Masada on Day 3). Herod's Masada fell to the Romans, but God's *metsudah* will never fail or falter or fall!

The psalmist then uses two sets of metaphors to describe God's protection from two kinds of enemies. The first are human enemies. The "snare" and "arrow" in verses 3–5 refer to threats launched against us by others. But an even greater danger, especially in Old Testament times, was that of "pestilence" (v. 6). This refers to plague and disease, unseen enemies that could seemingly attack randomly and without warning. In reminding his readers of God's protection, the writer stresses that God never goes off duty. He will protect against "the terror by night" or "the arrow that flies by day . . . the pestilence that stalks in darkness [and] the destruction that lays waste at noon" (vv. 5–6). Day or night, God protects His followers.

In the second half of the psalm the writer shows God giving His followers victory over the most deadly enemies, represented by the lion and the snake. "You will tread upon the lion and cobra, the young lion and the serpent you will trample down" (v. 13).

Nothing will harm you and no enemy can defeat you. Those are amazing promises. But are they true? What about the believer struggling with cancer? What about the followers of Christ being persecuted in the Middle East and other parts of the world? Is this psalm an ironclad promise from God, guaranteeing happiness and prosperity for all His followers?

Evidently Satan thought he could trick Jesus by suggesting this was the case. When he was tempting Jesus in the wilderness, Satan took Him to the pinnacle of the Temple and tried to tempt Jesus to jump off by quoting from this very psalm. "For He will give His angels charge concerning you, to guard you in all your ways. They will bear you up in their hands, that you do not strike your foot against a stone" (vv. 11–12, quoted by Satan in Matt. 4:5–6).

Jesus refused to fall into Satan's trap. To deliberately jump would have been to demand that God the Father serve Him, rather than the other way around. To put it into a modern metaphor, God might be our heavenly airbag—our protector—but that doesn't give us the right to deliberately drive our car into a tree!

But let me be even more clear. This passage isn't a heavenly insurance policy ensuring that we will never have problems or difficulties. Rather, it's a promise that when we face those times we have a shelter, a refuge (v. 2), a fortress (v. 2), a shield (v. 4), a bulwark (v. 4)—in short, a God in whom we can trust. Or, my favorite image of all, you have a loving protector who, like an eagle, will "cover you with His pinions [feathers]" so that "under His wings you may seek refuge" (v. 4).

**WALKING IN OUR LAND**

**TAKE ONE FINAL LOOK** toward the wilderness. It's definitely a place of trial and testing in the Bible. You might very well be facing your own spiritual wilderness right now. If you are, remember God's comforting promises in Psalm 91. To be a card-carrying member of the human race is to face problems and difficulties. But that same wilderness is also the place where God is waiting to take you under His wings to shelter and protect you.

Based, in part, on Psalm 91, William Cushing's hymn, *Under His Wings*, reminds us we are "sheltered, protected." Here are the words from verse 1; give thanks for these truths about our heavenly Father:

Under His wings I am safely abiding;
Though the night deepens and tempests are wild,
Still I can trust Him; I know He will keep me;
He has redeemed me, and I am His child.[1]

# Thanksgiving Recipes

## PSALM 96

Thanksgiving is the Super Bowl of festive eating! It's a time for roast turkey, baked pies, and multiple varieties of potatoes along with homemade gravy and all the other special salads and side dishes that make the day a family feast. Most would agree that Thanksgiving is a day to overindulge.

It seems every family has its own traditional recipes that help make Thanksgiving special. My favorite dish was my mom's pumpkin pie, a recipe my wife has also mastered. It's not too bland or too spicy. Every household is different, but nearly everyone has those special recipes that are part of their Thanksgiving memories.

Today I'd like to offer my own unique recipe to help make your next Thanksgiving special. No matter what your family traditions might be, this recipe will fit perfectly into your time of celebration. And the best part is that it involves no additional peeling, slicing, dicing, baking, boiling, or broiling. There are no additional pots or pans to be washed afterward. And it's calorie-free!

So what is this amazing recipe? It's actually a recipe on which *every* day ought to be based—a recipe for giving thanks to God.

In the midst of all the preparation and eating and cleanup and watching parades and football, the one thing that seems to be getting squeezed out of many Thanksgiving celebrations is the very reason the day was originally established—to give thanks to God.

We know the first Thanksgiving was celebrated by the Pilgrims in 1621, but few realize the first "official" Thanksgiving Day was proclaimed by President George Washington in 1789, during his very first year in office. He announced that Thursday, November 26, 1789, was to be set aside as "a day of Publick Thanksgiving and Prayer . . . to be observed by acknowledging with grateful hearts the many and signal favors of Almighty God."

Almost three thousand years earlier King David, the leader of Israel, issued his own thanksgiving proclamation. It's found in Psalm 96, and it contains the original recipe for thanksgiving that I want to share with you today.

Since the psalm doesn't identify its author, how do we know it was written by King David? The answer is found in 1 Chronicles 16. That passage contains an expanded version of Psalm 96. It begins with these words: "Then on that day David first assigned Asaph and his relatives to give thanks to the LORD" (v. 7). David commanded the temple singers to give thanks to God, and he supplied them with the first thanksgiving hymn they were to sing. That hymn, in a slightly modified form, made its way into Israel's national songbook as Psalm 96.

So what is the recipe for thanksgiving first shared by King David three thousand years ago? The recipe has

A group of children praying at the Western Wall in Jerusalem.

three parts, each of which contains an essential ingredient. Let's look at this recipe carefully.

David begins in verses 1–4 by saying we first need to thank God for *who He is*. He calls on all Israel to "Sing to the LORD a new song; sing to the LORD all the earth." We're to "bless His name" and "tell of His glory among the nations." But why should we do this? "For great is the LORD, and greatly to be praised."

All too often we think life is mainly about us. David begins by reminding his listeners that life is really all about God. We ought to give thanks to God for the simple reason that He is worthy of our praise. The Westminster Shorter Catechism states it this way: "Man's chief end is to glorify God, and to enjoy him forever." This ingredient of thanksgiving helps eliminate our own spiritual nearsightedness by reminding us to focus on God—and to thank Him for being who He is.

David then adds a second key ingredient, and it's probably the one we're most familiar with. He calls on his listeners to give thanks not only for who God is, but also for *what God is doing*. Using repetition to drive home his point, David encourages his audience to thank God for His continuing work on their behalf. "Ascribe to the LORD, O families of the peoples, ascribe to the LORD glory and strength. Ascribe to the LORD the glory of His name; bring an offering and come into His courts. Worship the LORD in holy attire; tremble before Him, all the earth. Say among the nations, 'The LORD reigns; indeed, the world is firmly established, it will not be moved'" (vv. 7–10).

Today we seem to be surrounded by signs of instability. Many of the things we've placed our trust in over the years now seem rather shaky. It's hard to think of banks or governments as being "rock solid." Seismic experts tell us even the rotation of the earth itself was changed by the earthquake that struck Japan several years ago.

But David says we can give thanks because our God *doesn't* change. His control over His creation is as firm today as it was the moment He formed it. Even when things around us appear to be in chaos, we can thank God for the reality that He is still seated on His throne in heaven—and still ruling over His creation.

Now some might have an objection here. If God is in control, they ask, how come we see such chaos and disruption in our world? Part of the answer rests in understanding that spiritual forces are at work around us that seek to oppose God and His plans. Yet even these forces have limits imposed by God Himself—limits on what they can do, and limits on how long they'll be allowed to continue.

After we thank God for who He is and for what He is doing, let's add the third ingredient to our Thanksgiving recipe: *what He will do in the future*. David ends his psalm by reminding his readers that God has a future already planned for His creation. Knowing the certainty of this future allows us to give thanks even when we haven't yet seen that actual outcome. David says it this way:

> He will judge the peoples with equity. Let the heavens be glad, and let the earth rejoice; let the sea roar, and all it contains; let the field exult, and all that is in it. Then all the trees of the forest will sing for joy before the Lord, for He is coming, for He is coming to judge the earth. He will judge the world in righteousness and the peoples in His faithfulness. (vv. 10–13)

This threefold recipe is reason enough to daily give thanks to our Lord.

**WALKING IN OUR LAND**

**WE CAN BE THANKFUL TODAY**—and every other day—because we know the end of the story. We've already read the last chapter of the Book! Revelation tells us Jesus is coming back to reign as King of kings and Lord of lords. God will reverse the curse on this earth, wipe away every tear from our eyes, and reward the faithfulness of His followers. And that's worth getting excited about!

At your next Thanksgiving, before you dig into the piles of mashed potatoes, bowls of dressing, and heaps of turkey, pause and give thanks to God. But don't *just* thank Him for the food before you, for the family and friends, as delightful as all that is. Instead, start by thanking Him for being the God of the universe. And then thank Him for His control over everything in creation, even when we can't fully understand all that's taking place. Finally, thank Him for the fact that Jesus is coming again. And after you thank Him for food, family, and friends, end your prayer of thanksgiving the same way the apostle John ended the book of Revelation. "Amen. Come, Lord Jesus."

Come to think of it, why wait until Thanksgiving? Why not thank Him today?

# The "Old Hundredth"

## PSALM 100

Yesterday's psalm of thanksgiving brought to our senses the sights, sounds, and smells of a traditional Thanksgiving holiday; today's psalm continues our thanksgiving theme. For Christians, any day ought to be a good day to sing the Doxology:

Praise God, from whom all blessings flow;
Praise Him, all creatures here below;
Praise Him above, ye heavenly host;
Praise Father, Son, and Holy Ghost. Amen.[1]

As you read those words, perhaps you can even hear the melody of the Doxology in your head. The music comes from a hymn tune known as the "Old Hundredth." That sounds like an unusual title for a melody until you realize that the tune received its name from its association with the psalm we're looking at today: Psalm 100. The tune was written in the early sixteenth century, and the words we sing today were composed by a clergyman in the Church of England in 1674.

Psalm 100 is an anonymous psalm written to give thanks to God. After yesterday's psalm of thanksgiving it seems appropriate to pause and reflect on the hows and whys of giving thanks that are presented in Psalm 100—the *original* "old hundredth." The psalm is short, just five verses long. But like the Doxology, it packs a lot of truth into that short amount of space. It actually has two stanzas. Verses 1–3 form the first stanza and verses 4–5 the second. And in each stanza the psalmist first tells us *how* to give thanks and then tells us *why* to give thanks.

The inscription to the psalm is very straightforward. "A Psalm for Thanksgiving." The Hebrew word for "thanksgiving" is *todah*. This happens to be one of the Hebrew words every traveler to Israel should learn. When a member of the wait staff refills the water bottle on the table or someone holds open a door, it's appropriate to say to them *todah*—"Thank you." In essence, the inscription says this is a psalm for saying thank you to God.

The psalm begins by commanding all the earth to "shout joyfully to the LORD." The word "joyfully" isn't expressly present in the Hebrew text, but here shouting

Zion Gate, one of the eight gates in the walls surrounding Jerusalem.

conveys the idea of shouting joyfully or triumphantly. It's the cry of a victor. "Yes! Huzzah! We did it!" It's the jubilation we experience when our team scores the winning goal, the sense of joy and excitement that makes us jump to our feet and shout out. That's how the writer begins this psalm.

The psalmist then narrows that sense of excitement to a laser-like focus. He calls on his readers to "serve the LORD with gladness." The word for "serve" actually comes from the word for toil or work. The imagery here reminds me of Jacob's bargain with Laban to serve seven years for Rachel. He did the work, but it "seemed to him but a few days because of his love for her" (Gen. 29:20). We not only shout in triumph, but we also serve in joy.

The "service" the psalmist has in mind is most likely Israel's gathering at the Temple in Jerusalem to worship God. When they made their pilgrimage to Jerusalem, the people weren't to see it as a burden or hardship. It took effort, but it was a labor of love and joy. This can be seen in the writer's description of them breaking out in song, expressing their heartfelt worship of God: "Come before Him with joyful singing" (v. 2).

That's *how* we're to give thanks to God. But *why* should we do so? The psalmist ends the first stanza by explaining why God deserves our thanks. He deserves our thanks because He's our *Creator* and He's our *Sustainer*. As Creator He made us, and that also gives Him right of ownership over us. But He's not some evil overlord brutally controlling His possession. The psalmist instead uses the image of a shepherd and his sheep. God is the loving shepherd who watches over "the sheep of His pasture" (v. 3). He is our owner, but as such He is the Good Shepherd of Psalm 23, who protects and shows us compassion (see Day 6).

In the second stanza the psalmist rehearses the same two themes. How are we to worship God? We're to "enter His gates with thanksgiving and His courts with praise" and to "give thanks to Him" and "bless His name" (v. 4). We can't impart a blessing to God, so what does it mean to "bless His name"? We bless God by expressing to Him our gratitude and appreciation. When God is the object, the Hebrew word for bless might best be translated "praise." The psalmist calls on the people to enter God's house expressing deep thankfulness and open praise.

But if that's *how* we are to say thank you to God, *why* is it so important to do so? The psalmist says it's important not only because of what God has done, but also because of who He is. "For the LORD is good" (v. 5). The Hebrew word for good is *tov*, and it summarizes the essential goodness of God. When Satan first came to tempt Adam and Eve, he began by questioning God's goodness. "Indeed, has God said, 'You shall not eat from any tree of the garden'?" (Gen. 3:1). To doubt God's goodness is to doubt His very being.

The psalmist gives two practical illustrations of God's essential goodness. First, he says that His "lovingkindness is everlasting." How good is God? He promised you an eternal destiny, and He will keep His promise until you finally arrive at your eternal home. Then, the psalmist reminds his readers that God's "faithfulness" extends "to all generations." Another word for faithfulness is trustworthiness, and the writer affirms that the God who could be counted on by Abraham, or David, or the Maccabees, or Mary and Joseph is just as trustworthy today. His warranty never expires!

**WALKING IN OUR LAND**

**SOMETIME TODAY** do something that might be just a little out of character for you. Pause, look toward heaven, and then start belting out the Doxology at full volume. Sing out because God is your Creator, because He cares for you day by day, because He's good, because His loyal love to you will never end, and because He's always trustworthy.

When you have sung the final word—"Amen"—say it to God once more, for it is true. And all God's people said, "Amen!"

# Comfort Amid Conflict

## PSALM 102

As a tour leader in the Holy Land, I've found that the first day of a trip to Israel is usually the hardest—but for reasons you might not expect.

The group is fresh, excited, ready to explore the land. Our first stop is usually Caesarea, and that's where the group starts snapping photos nonstop! I don't blame them. Caesarea is a fantastic site, and it's probably the first time most have ever seen a two-thousand-year-old theater, a hippodrome, a Roman aqueduct, or the ruins of a palace built by the Bible's very own Herod the Great. The problem is that they want to spend *hours* at Caesarea, while I know all of the other sites we have yet to visit. If they dawdle here, they could miss the last site of the day—Mount Arbel—which is truly spectacular!

Mount Arbel is part of Israel's National Park system, which means it has a set closing time. If you arrive too late, the gate to the parking lot will be closed and locked for the night. But even if you arrive before closing, there's a limited window of time for you to make it to the summit without missing the beautiful panorama before you. Ideally you want to arrive as the sun is going down but while it's still high enough in the sky to be shining on the mountain. For about an hour the cliff face takes on a golden hue and the ever-lengthening shadows cause each ridge and undulation to stand out in sharp contrast. The mountains in the distance remain distinct from the darkening blue of the sky and a thousand feet below the land bordering the Sea of Galilee takes on a warm bronze glow.

Mount Arbel with the Sea of Galilee in the background.

Sadly, a delay of only thirty minutes can make all the difference. As the sun drops closer toward the horizon, the mountains to the west start to block its rays. The golden cliffs turn a muddy shade of gray, as the shadows reach out and cover the entire landscape. The panorama is still there, but its beauty has faded like an old photograph. First-time tourists arriving late don't know what they've missed, but I do, and that's why I keep them moving all day!

Walking down the trail of Mount Arbel as the sun dips toward the horizon always reminds me of the words of Psalm 102. "My days are like a lengthened shadow" (v. 11). In fact, let's pause here and look briefly at this psalm. The deepening shadows in the canyon below us can serve as the backdrop for our study.

We don't know who wrote this psalm or when. But the introduction tells us much about how the writer was feeling as he penned it: "A Prayer of the Afflicted when he is faint and pours out his complaint before the LORD." The psalm is clearly a cry for help from someone experiencing deep pain and anguish.

The psalmist begins his prayer by pleading with God. No fancy phrases or flowery language. There's no time to waste. It's as if he is saying urgently, "I need your help, Lord. Now!"

So what's the problem? At first we don't know. But whatever it is, the stress is actually causing physical illness. In verses 3–11 the writer describes his symptoms to the heavenly Physician. He begins and ends this section by describing his life as withering away. "My days have been consumed in smoke" (v. 3). "My days are like a lengthened shadow" (v. 11). Like a puff of smoke rising into the sky, or a shadow reaching out to consume the few remaining patches of sunshine, the writer feels his life is evaporating before his very eyes. He forgets to eat (v. 4), and he's losing so much weight that he's reduced to skin and bones (v. 5). And these physical changes have been accompanied by intense feelings of loneliness. He cries out that he feels like an owl in the desert (v. 6) or a "lonely bird on a housetop" (v. 7). The psalmist is alone, anxious, and depressed.

What could cause such intense pain and heartache? The psalmist hints at the root cause in verses 13–21. He longs for the day when God will again "have compassion on Zion" (v. 13), rebuild the city, and reappear there in His glory. This will be a time when nations and kings will once again "fear the name of the LORD" (v. 15) and revere Him. From these clues it seems likely the psalm was written during the Babylonian exile, a time when the people of Judah were held in captivity. This was a time when the city of Jerusalem and temple of Solomon sat in ruins. The writer might have been one of the early exiles who had just received word of the city's destruction. Perhaps he was even being mocked by his Babylonian tormentors, who were merciless in reminding the Jewish exiles of their loss (cf. Ps. 137:1–3).

We might not know exactly why this writer is so discouraged, but we've all experienced similar times of discouragement in our own lives. So what's the solution to such crushing sadness? Thankfully, the psalmist provides the answer.

Three different times in this psalm the writer turns from his own problems to gaze into the face of God. After announcing in verse 11 how his days seemed to be as fleeting as a "lengthened shadow" (or "evening shadow," NIV), the writer immediately added, "But You, O LORD, abide forever" (v. 12). Our lives here on earth are temporal, but God is eternal.

A few verses later the writer focuses on God's power in creating the heavens and the earth. "Of old You founded the earth, and the heavens are the work of Your hands" (v. 25). But he quickly adds in verse 26, "Even they will perish." Everything around us that seems so permanent—including our problems—won't last forever. Only God is eternal. "But You are the same, and Your years will not come to an end" (v. 27).

So how did the psalmist find comfort in the midst of conflict? He did so by focusing on the character of God. Problems are temporary, but God abides forever. Circumstances can change, but God will always remain the same.

**WALKING IN OUR LAND**

**THE SUN IS ABOUT TO SLIP** below the horizon, and the temperature is starting to drop, so it's time to head back toward the bus. But as we do, think about the lessons of Psalm 102. I don't know what problems you might be facing today, but God does. More than that, He cares deeply for you and wants you to bring your burdens to Him . . . to seek out His care, help, comfort, and compassion.

Yes, at times it is hard to hand your burdens over to the Lord. Events and uncertainty fog our perspective. At such times we need to follow the example of the psalmist. Shift your gaze from yourself to Him. He's the God of sovereign power who will "abide forever" (v. 12). He's the God of infinite love who promises to "have compassion" and "be gracious" (v. 13). Most important of all, He's the God who answers prayer, who "looked down from His holy height . . . to hear the groaning of the prisoner [and] set free those who were doomed to death" (vv. 19–20). The psalmist is reminding us that God hears, He cares, and He has the power to carry us through!

# A Song for the Mount of Olives

## PSALM 118

**M**any Christians have their own favorite choruses or hymns—songs that connect them emotionally to a special time or place in their relationship with God. Just hearing the opening notes can bring back a flood of memories. Today we will look at a song from Israel's songbook that will forever link the Mount of Olives with Jesus.

As we walk down the roadway away from the top of the Mount of Olives, we see the Kidron Valley in front of us. Watch your step! This is a steep decline, and I don't want you to slip on any loose gravel. I'll bet you're glad we're walking *down* rather than *up* the hill!

This is the very route Jesus walked on His triumphal entry into Jerusalem. Now imagine the roadway we're traveling completely packed with Jewish pilgrims making their way to Jerusalem to celebrate Passover. A rumor sweeps through the crowd that Jesus—Yeshua, the miracle worker—is on His way over the hill from Bethany. Everyone stops and begins looking back up the hill. Their patience is rewarded when they spot a man sitting on a young colt, surrounded by a shouting throng.

As the group approaches, a familiar refrain rises from the gathered crowd: "Blessed is the one who comes in the name of the LORD" (Ps. 118:26). Psalm 118 was one of the psalms sung at each of the major festivals when Israel gathered before the Lord.

And then something clicks in several pilgrims' minds as they think back over some of the other phrases in that psalm. "The stone which the builders rejected has become the chief corner stone" (v. 22). The religious leaders have already rejected Jesus, but could even that rejection mirror the words of this prophetic psalm? Could Jesus indeed be the One pictured in this psalm?

As these pilgrims watch the crowd placing palm branches on the roadway, still another phrase from the psalm comes to their minds. "With boughs in hand, join in the festal procession up to the horns of the altar" (v. 27b NIV) As the crowd passes by, the group of curious travelers follow along and find themselves turning Psalm 118 over in their minds.

Those thoughts fade as the week progresses. Soon groups of family members focus on all the preparations for

Passover. There's so much to do to get ready. Then comes the celebration itself as they gather together in the city to rehearse the miracle of God's deliverance from Egypt. The celebration ends with the family singing Psalm 118, and that's when several remember the events earlier in the week on the Mount of Olives. "Blessed is the one who comes in the name of the LORD" (v. 26). Could there indeed be a connection?

After the Passover celebration, some of the men step outside into the cool night air. As they glance toward a

Walking down the Mount of Olives with the walls of Jerusalem in the distance.

nearby home, they see lights flickering through a window in its upper chamber. Another family is concluding its celebration of Passover, and again the strains of Psalm 118 can be heard. A figure of a man passes in front of the window. The light from the oil lamps in the room is very dim, but aided by the full moon those below feel as if they know Him. Why, it looks like Yeshua, the man on the donkey! A few moments later the group emerges from the house, and one of the men tells another they will be spending the night on the Mount of Olives . . . at the olive oil press—*gat shemen*—Gethsemane.

The male observers walk back inside, but they can't stop thinking about Psalm 118, a psalm of thanks for God's deliverance. It's a psalm that begins and ends with the same theme: "Give thanks to the Lord, for He is good; for His lovingkindness is everlasting" (vv. 1, 29). Twice this week these pilgrims have connected the psalm with Jesus, first on the Mount of Olives and now outside this Upper Room as He and His disciples headed back to the Mount of Olives. Those two connections by themselves would certainly make this psalm special, memorable. But the story isn't over.

Jesus came as Israel's Messiah, and Psalm 118 was one of the Old Testament spotlights that pointed prophetically to Him. But less than a week after the events on

Palm Sunday those who had shouted "Blessed is He who comes in the name of the LORD" (John 12:13), would cry instead, "Crucify Him! . . . We have no king but Caesar" (19:15). Yet this turn of events didn't take Jesus—or God the Father—by surprise. In fact, during that final week Jesus announced to the city, "Jerusalem, Jerusalem, who kills the prophets and stones those who are sent to her! How often I wanted to gather your children together, the way a hen gathers her chicks under her wings, and you were unwilling. Behold, your house is being left to you desolate! For I say to you, from now on you will not see Me until you say, 'Blessed is He who comes in the name of the LORD!'" (Matt. 23:37–39).

And there's our key passage again! Psalm 118 will be sung a third time in Jerusalem at the Mount of Olives. But this time, those who are singing will be doing so in true faith as they welcome the *return* of the Messiah. That's the day the prophet Zechariah said the Messiah's feet will again stand on the Mount of Olives, which will be split in half. It's the day he said they will "look on Me whom they have pierced; and they will mourn for Him, as one mourns for an only son" (Zech. 12:10). It's the day when the stone once rejected by the builders will indeed become the chief cornerstone, just as Psalm 118 predicted!

"Blessed is the one who comes in the name of the Lord!" The song that was number one during the final week of Christ's ministry will again be number one . . . when He returns as king!

**WALKING IN OUR LAND**

**AS WE LEAVE THE MOUNT OF OLIVES**, it's important to remember that God's plan for His Son always anticipated the cross before the crown. It always placed Calvary before the kingdom. In Psalm 118 God said the stone would be rejected before it became the chief cornerstone. God's plan at Christ's first coming was fulfilled exactly as predicted in the Bible, even if it wasn't fully understood by His followers.

Take time to read through Psalm 118 with a focus on Jesus. Then pause and thank the Father for sending His Son to die for you—and for His *promise* that Jesus will someday return again. Finally, with the psalmist, add to your prayer of thanksgiving to the Father this exclamation: "Blessed is the one who comes in the name of the Lord!"

# Solitary Prayers in Lonely Places

## PSALM 120

A Holy Land tour is one of the few places where it is possible to have dinner in a Bedouin tent. But before dinner, how would you like to go on a camel ride? Since I've already ridden a camel, I'll stay here to guard all your belongings as you "swing and sway" on your ship of the desert. But do me one favor. See if you can snap any pictures of a broom tree during your desert safari. You're looking for a green shrub about five to ten feet tall that appears to be covered in pine needles.

Back so soon? Well, that's good because it's almost time for dinner, Bedouin style! Take a look at the cooking fire. The black, inverted saucer perched above it is the cooktop. You can already see the flatbread cooking there. And off to the side is the coffee pot where they're boiling the Arabic coffee. You can have my share! Trust me, a little goes a long way.

Now, look more closely at the fire. See those red hot coals? They almost remind you of charcoal burning in a grill. But these "briquettes" are actually wood from the broom trees you saw out in the wilderness. That wood is hard and dense, and it creates a very hot fire.

The sun has gone down, and you're starting to feel the chill of the night air. So gather closely around this warm fire as we look at solitary prayers from lonely places. Our passage for this study is Psalm 120, the first of a collection of psalms known as the Songs (or Psalms) of Ascents.

These fifteen psalms, from 120 through 134, were composed at different times by different writers. But at some

Preparing bread and coffee in a Bedouin encampment. *Inset:* A cooking fire ablaze at the entrance to a Bedouin tent.

point they were collected and grouped together. Most likely, the collection process took place after the Babylonian captivity. The title "Songs of Ascents" was likely given to the collection because these psalms were to be sung by Jewish pilgrims during the three annual feasts when they "ascended" or came up to Jerusalem to gather before God. Psalm 120 was placed at the head of the parade, the first of the psalms these pilgrims were to recite.

We would expect these journeys to Jerusalem to be joyous occasions since the pilgrims were on their way to the Temple. But Psalm 120 begins by focusing not on the happiness that was ahead but on the heartache surrounding the writer on all sides. Let's peer over the shoulder of this unknown psalmist as he cries out in prayer to God. "In my trouble I cried to the LORD, and He answered me" (v. 1).

Okay, just a small grammar lesson for verse 1. Hebrew doesn't have past, present, or future tenses; they need to be supplied by the context. So we face an immediate translation problem here. Is the psalmist saying he cried and God answered—actions that have already taken place— or is he saying, "In my trouble I cry to the LORD and he answers," suggesting he is in the middle of the problem and anticipating God's answer momentarily? From the overall context of the psalm, I think the second option is the better translation. The psalmist is facing a challenge and calling out to God for help. But even as he does so, he knows by faith that God will respond.

This first verse summarizes the entire psalm; in verses 2–4 the psalmist provides more detail about the trouble he is facing. He asks God to deliver him from "lying lips" and a "deceitful tongue" (v. 2). These are figures of speech. After all, the lips and the tongue don't do anything by themselves. It's the person telling the lips and tongue what to do who is ultimately responsible! The word "deceitful" conveys the idea of "beguiling or misleading." We're not sure if these evil people are lying *to* the psalmist or lying *about* the psalmist, though the second seems most likely. It's possible they were spreading vicious rumors about him.

If you've ever had anyone slander you, or lie about you, or try to deceive others into believing harmful and hurtful things about you, then you know how the psalmist felt. He asks God to judge the evil person in an appropriate way. The enemy's slanderous words were like arrows piercing into the psalmist's innermost being, or—recalling the image of our Bedouin friend at his campfire—like burning embers searing his very soul. So he warns his enemy that God was about to shoot "sharp arrows" back at him and burn him with the "burning coals of the broom tree" (v. 4). And that's why we've come *here*!

Let's pause to look again at the Bedouin fire. Those hot, glowing coals come from the broom tree, and they're a great object lesson. The psalmist is under attack, but he refuses to lash back. Instead, he commits the situation to God, whose white-hot sense of justice and righteousness guarantees that eventually the wicked will be punished and the righteous will be vindicated. The psalmist might not know exactly *when*, but he's confident God will balance the scales of justice at the proper time.

We've all faced times of loneliness and heartache when we've been slandered, maligned, or unfairly attacked. The psalmist is reminding us that in those times we can call out to God and be assured that He's listening. Now, that doesn't mean He will always intervene according to our timetable. In fact, look carefully at what the psalmist says next.

"Woe is me, for I sojourn in Meshech, for I dwell among the tents of Kedar! Too long has my soul had its dwelling with those who hate peace" (vv. 5–6). The psalmist is using poetic language—but real places—to describe his condition. Meshech was far to the north of Israel, in central Asia, while Kedar was far to the southeast, on the Arabian Peninsula. The psalmist uses these distant lands to describe his own sense of alienation and exile from that place of security we all know as home. Like Dorothy trapped in Oz, the psalmist wants to tap his heels together and cry out, "There's no place like home!" He longs for peace, but his adversaries continually want to fight and do battle.

## WALKING IN OUR LAND

**BUT WHAT DOES THIS** psalmist's cry for help have to do with us? If you ever enter a Bedouin tent, the first thing you'll notice is it's not a permanent structure. The walls are made of goats' hair; the floors are dirt covered by thin carpets. Similarly, when the psalmist said he felt as if he were dwelling in those foreign lands, he used words that indicate a temporary dwelling, words that can be translated "sojourn" and "tabernacle." He felt unsettled, but that's because he wasn't yet home. And as you journey through life, there will be times when you'll be misunderstood and maligned by those who don't like you, and others who might even want to harm you. This psalm provides three specific ways for us to make it through those times.

First, we are reminded to *pray and share our struggles with God*. "In my trouble I cried to the LORD" (v. 1). Second, we are encouraged to *turn our problems over to God and ask for his deliverance in due season.*

"Deliver me, O LORD," (v. 2). Rather than becoming a prisoner to anger or bitterness, we can let God dispense His justice in His proper time. Finally, we are told that we're not yet home (v. 5). Like Israel in the wilderness, we're just sojourners in this life on our way to a heavenly Promised Land. Much like the description of Abraham in Hebrews 11:9–10, we might have a sense of incompleteness today, but that's because we're still "looking for the city which has foundations, whose architect and builder is God."

The next time you're struggling because someone has mistreated you, don't lash out. Instead, recall to your mind the hot, burning coals of the broom tree and remember that God will resolve the issue at the appropriate time—as long as you're willing to hand your problems over to Him!

# A Disturbing Question with a Reassuring Answer

## PSALM 121

The first Christian artwork I ever remember seeing featured a beautiful photograph of Glacier National Park. Several snow-capped mountain peaks pushed their way into a dazzling blue sky. Below the peaks was a lush valley, forested in green, with a stream carving its way through the middle. And at the bottom of the picture was a quotation from Psalm 121:1: "I will lift up mine eyes unto the hills, from whence cometh my help" (KJV).

The photo and verse seemed so well matched. As a relatively new Christian I could envision God sitting atop His heavenly mountain, divine binoculars in hand, keeping watch on His followers below. Whenever I felt alone, or threatened, I could remember those majestic heights and know God was watching, ready to ride to my rescue if needed.

This picture was a beautiful and inspiring piece of art.

Unfortunately, it was based on a total misunderstanding of Psalm 121! That verse is asking a question, *not* making a statement, as this particular Bible version had it. (The ESV, NASB, NIV, and NKJV translations have it right). The mountains represent hidden dangers, not God's heavenly deliverance. To understand this psalm, we need to join a group of pilgrims traveling to Jerusalem for one of Israel's annual feasts.

Three times each year God called on Israel to appear before Him—at the Feasts of Passover, Pentecost, and Tabernacles. Once Solomon's temple was completed, the destination for the journey was Jerusalem. And it was quite a journey! Twenty-seven times in the Old and New Testaments the Bible talks about going *up* to Jerusalem. That's an accurate expression because Jerusalem is located in the hill country. A trip to Jerusalem was a journey up into the mountains.

Imagine what it might have been like to take part in one of those pilgrimages. Though God only required the men to appear before Him (Ex. 23:17), entire families made the trip. Dr. Luke, the gospel writer, tells us that Jesus' parents "went to Jerusalem every year at the Feast of the Passover" (Luke 2:41), so mother and son accompanied Joseph on the journey. When it came time to travel to Jerusalem, extended families and perhaps entire villages set out on the journey. Towns might have been left virtually deserted and unguarded.

But it's not what we're leaving behind that's weighing on our mind as we begin our journey. It's what might be lurking ahead that has us concerned. We stare ahead at the hills in the distance. Just beyond those peaks are more hills, followed still by others. The terrain is rough and rocky and full of hard climbs on treacherous paths. This journey involved alternately baking under a relentless sun by day and shivering under a cloudless sky by night. We might encounter bears, lions, poisonous snakes, or scorpions. Perhaps most frightening of all, there could be

Looking up to the hills of the Judean Wilderness.

two-legged threats waiting in remote areas to attack the unsuspecting, the weak, and the vulnerable.

The pilgrimage to Jerusalem was a journey of faith, but it could also be very dangerous, and that's what prompted the psalmist to ask his alarming question at the beginning of Psalm 121. "I will lift up my eyes to the mountains. From where shall my help come?" How can I hope to make it safely through the mountains to and from Jerusalem?

Psalm 121 is the second in this group of fifteen psalms collectively labeled as "Songs of Ascents," psalms sung by the pilgrims as they "ascended" to Jerusalem for the three annual feasts. Certainly Psalm 121 gives voice to the angst felt by every pilgrim beginning that long and treacherous trek as they wondered, *Where can I find the help I need to overcome all these obstacles?*

Thankfully, the psalmist immediately provides a reassuring answer to his disturbing question. "My help comes from the LORD, who made heaven and earth" (v. 2). The writer's problems, represented by the mountains, might indeed loom large, but he quickly reminds himself—and us—that God is far greater than whatever problems we might face. He is reliable. The psalmist then provided three reassuring reasons God is so reliable.

In verses 3–4 the psalmist describes God as an ever-watchful shepherd. Multiple times the psalmist assures the pilgrims of God's sleepless vigil. "He who keeps you will not slumber. . . . He who keeps Israel will neither slumber nor sleep." God never goes off duty. Instead, He promises to stand guard and "not allow your foot to slip."

In verses 5–6 the psalmist reminds us that God is an ever-vigilant champion, standing by the pilgrim's right hand to protect him. "The sun will not smite you by day, nor the moon by night." God guards His followers from the blazing heat of the day and from the sinister forces that lurk in the night. He's always by our side.

Finally, in verses 7–8 the psalmist affirms that God is the everlasting protector. He will "guard your going out and your coming in." God not only promised to take care of those coming to worship Him in Jerusalem, but He also vowed to watch over them as they traveled back home as well. And the psalmist says God's protection will last "from this time forth and forever." It extended beyond the journey to Jerusalem to encompass the rest of the pilgrim's journey through life.

Though our struggles are real, never forget that God is greater than any problems we face. If you have your Bible, open it to Psalm 121 and circle (or highlight) the following phrases. Five times the writer uses a figure of speech called a *merism*, which combines two contrasting words in order to stress the totality or completeness of God's protection. In verse 2: God is the maker of *heaven and earth*; in verse 6: He protects against *the sun and the moon*, and does so *by day and night*; in verse 8: He watches over *your going out and your coming in*, and He promises to do so both *now* ("This time forth") *and forever*.

Second, underline the words "keep," "protect," and "guard." These are all translations of the same Hebrew word, which is used six times in these eight verses. This seeming repetition is intended to emphasize that the all-powerful, ever-vigilant God of the universe is the One who promises to stand guard over our lives.

**WALKING IN OUR LAND**

**ARE YOU STARING AT LIFE'S MOUNTAINS**, wondering if you have the strength to make it through? Psalm 121 has your answer. Look beyond the obstacles in your path and focus on the God who made heaven and earth—the God who promises to watch over and care for those who follow after Him.

Mildred Leightner Dillon and her husband William ministered to thousands of Chicago's inner-city poor and homeless while working for the Sunshine Gospel Mission. Hundreds of Moody Bible Institute students have worked with this mission over the years. But Mildred and William also found time to write and arrange music. In fact, Mildred wrote a song entitled "Safe Am I" that blends the truth of Psalm 121 with the promise made by Jesus in John 10. This message of hope still resonates with anyone facing life's threats. Why not make Psalm 121, along with the words of this short chorus, your theme for today?

> Safe am I, safe am I,
> In the hollow of His hand;
> Sheltered o'er, sheltered o'er,
> With His love forever more.
> No ill can harm me, no foe alarm me,
> For He keeps both day and night;
> Safe am I, safe am I,
> In the hollow of His hand.[1]

# The Peace of Jerusalem

## PSALM 122

It's hard to explain the emotional impact a trip to Israel has on a person. Mark Twain captured the feeling as well as anyone. He rode into the Holy Land on horseback, and the first place he visited connected to the life of Jesus was Caesarea Philippi. That experience led America's premier humorist to a moment of profound contemplation. "I can not comprehend yet that I am sitting where a god has stood, and looking upon the brook and the mountains which that god looked upon, and am surrounded by dusky men and women whose ancestors saw him, and even talked with him, face to face, and carelessly, just as they would have done with any other stranger. I can not comprehend this."[1]

Such feelings of deep spiritual and emotional connectedness seem to increase as the pilgrim gets closer to Jerusalem, the city that lies at the heart of God's past and future plan for His creation. In fact, the emotional impact can become so overwhelming that it has even resulted in psychological problems for some who aren't equipped to handle it. The phenomenon has become known as Jerusalem Syndrome, and it causes such individuals to experience intense religious feelings to the point where they believe God is speaking to them or announcing that they're to be His messengers to proclaim His impending return. Though no one on my trips has dealt with this, it is a serious condition with potential to harm the sufferer or those around them.

View of the Eastern Gate from the Kidron Valley.

I mention this anecdote because nearly everyone who travels to the Holy Land should understand the emotional impact of visiting the city—and how it has the potential to overwhelm a visitor.

That emotional impact isn't new, nor is it limited to those traveling from outside the country. In fact, King David described the same feelings in Psalm 122, a song he wrote to commemorate those times when Israel gathered in his new capital to worship God. The psalm David penned was later included in the Songs of Ascents.

David began Psalm 122 by expressing a pilgrim's

anticipation and excitement upon visiting Jerusalem—
the city where God dwelt among His people. "I was glad
when they said to me, 'Let us go to the house of the
Lord.' Our feet are standing within your gates, O Jerusalem." I can hear the excitement in David's voice. And
as he switches from the singular "*I* was glad" to the plural
"Let *us* go up . . . *our* feet are standing," it's as if he extends his arms to embrace everyone arriving in the city.
His words become *their* words as they all shared in the
excitement of the visit.

But having described this excitement in the first two
verses, David quickly redirects our focus. This isn't about
*us*; rather, it's about God and the place He has chosen. In
the next three verses David shifts our attention toward
the city and its significance.

Jerusalem's importance didn't just come from its physical appearance. When David described it as "a city that
is compact together" (v. 3), he wasn't describing just its
size. Behind the word for "compact" is the idea of "being
bound together" that likely represents the spiritual unity
of the people as much as the tight physical arrangement
of the city's houses and walls.

Jerusalem was David's capital city, yet its true import
was given to the city by God. God had commanded the
people of Israel to appear before Him three times each

year "at the place which He will choose" (Deut. 31:11). And the city God ultimately selected was Jerusalem. It was the place, David says, "to which the tribes go up, even the tribes of the LORD—an ordinance for Israel—to give thanks to the name of the LORD" (v. 4).

Jerusalem was also the city selected by God to be the capital of the united kingdom of Israel from which His chosen king would reign. It was the place where "the thrones of the house of David" were set up. Jerusalem was the city where God visibly dwelt among His people and the city from which God's anointed ruler led them.

Having explained the joy with which people were streaming to this city, David ended his song by calling on these visitors to pray for the city. In verses 6 and 7 he explained *what* they're to pray for, and in verses 8–9 he explained *why* those prayers are so important. All visitors were asked to pray for both peace and security. "Pray for the peace of Jerusalem. . . . May peace be within your walls" (vv. 6–7). The word "peace" here—*shalom*—is more than just an absence of war or violence. It refers to the health, wholeness, soundness, and prosperity of the city. These pilgrims were to pray that Jerusalem would experience all the blessing and security one would associate with a right relationship to God.

David ended his psalm with a practical application

explaining *why* these pilgrims were to pray for the peace of Jerusalem. First, it would benefit "my brothers and my friends" (v. 8). Peaceful conditions allowed pilgrims to continue to fulfill their obligation to gather before God. A spiritually healthful environment within the city also allowed the kings to rule in a righteous way.

But second, David explains that peace would benefit God's program here on earth. "For the sake of the house of the LORD our God, I will seek your good" (v. 9). In many ways David's words at the end of Psalm 122 parallel Paul's words in 1 Timothy 2:1–4. "First of all, then, I urge that entreaties and prayers, petitions and thanksgivings, be made on behalf of all men, for kings and all who are in authority, so that we may lead a tranquil and quiet life in all godliness and dignity. This is good and acceptable in the sight of God our Savior, who desires all men to be saved and to come to the knowledge of the truth." Our prayers for peace—for tranquil, quiet lives—are pleasing to God and help keep His good news from being hindered.

## WALKING IN OUR LAND

**LIVING IN THE TWENTY-FIRST CENTURY,** how can we pray for the peace of Jerusalem? Let me suggest two ways based on what we learned from today's psalm. First, if you're not already doing so, consider *praying regularly* for the peace of Jerusalem, for its wholeness and prosperity. Pray for the sake of the Jewish people—and God's program for the future; ask God to work in special ways to pour out His physical and spiritual *shalom* on that special place.

Second, go to God in prayer and ask Him if He wants *you* to travel to the Holy Land and visit Jerusalem. It was a transforming experience in David's day, and it can have the same impact on people today. His answer might be "No," or "Not right now." But I would challenge you to pray about it, because He might just open the door and provide the way for you to go!

# God's Geography Lesson

## PSALM 125

Today's walk takes us outside the historic walled city of Jerusalem . . . to the *original* city of Jerusalem. The current walls extend nearly three miles around the old city of Jerusalem, rising to a height of fifty feet. But as beautiful and iconic as they are, they fail to enclose the entire area that was once the biblical city of Jerusalem. Part of the Western Hill, now mistakenly called Mount Zion, was left outside the walls, and so was the hill on which the original city of Jerusalem once stood.

Many visitors are surprised to learn that the current Old City walls are only approaching their five hundreth birthday. In America, something five hundred years old sounds ancient. But in a city that already existed when Abraham walked through the land four thousand years ago, these walls are relatively recent. But these "recent" walls don't encompass the hill on which David established his capital.

After exiting the Old City through the current Dung Gate, we come to the City of David archaeological park and from there we will head up to the observation platform. There's much we can see and do here, but our time is limited so let's first take in the view. We begin by looking down at the original City of David itself. We're actually standing on the highest part of the small hill on

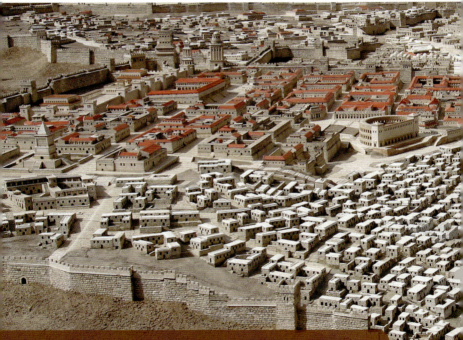

A model of Jerusalem as it may have looked during the time of Jesus. The location of the original City of David is visible on the lower right, and the Temple dominates just above the original city. Today the Dome of the Rock sits where the Temple once stood.

which the earliest city of Jerusalem stood. Clearly, it was quite small. Yet the Bible refers to it as the *stronghold* of David (2 Sam. 5:7–9), which is an apt description. But look farther to the south. See that hill rising up in the distance? It's sometimes called the Hill of Evil Counsel, because it's the traditional spot where Caiaphas and his colleagues decided to arrest Jesus.

Now turn toward the east. The deep valley in front of us is the Kidron Valley, and the mountain just beyond is the Mount of Olives. Like the Hill of Evil Counsel, the Mount of Olives is higher than the platform on which we're standing.

Now turn again and look north. We are now facing the Temple Mount and the gray dome of the al-Aqsa Mosque. From here we get a true sense of how much higher is the elevation of Mount Moriah, where the Temple once stood.

Finally, turn one last time to face west. Rising above us is the western hill, the one mistakenly called Mount Zion today. In fact, no matter which way we turn, the mountains surrounding us are higher than the hill on which we're standing. Jerusalem was built on this hill because it had the water supply, but the hill itself isn't nearly as high as any of the surrounding mountains.

And now it's time to look closely at Psalm 125, another of the Songs of Ascents. This psalm begins with two geography lessons from God. The first lesson is found in verse 1. "Those who trust in the LORD are as Mount Zion, which cannot be moved but abides forever." The "Mount Zion" mentioned here is not the modern Mount Zion, the western hill. Rather, the psalmist is referring to the original city of Jerusalem along with the adjacent

Temple Mount. That would have encompassed the spot where we're standing . . . and the area just to the north and south. And ultimately, this mention of the permanence of these hills is a reminder of the permanence of God's care for those who put their trust in Him.

The second geography lesson follows immediately afterward, in verse 2. "As the mountains surround Jerusalem, so the LORD surrounds His people from this time forth and forever." This verse is a perfect illustration of why it's so valuable to see the geographical context of Scripture. In this spot, no matter which way we turn we are looking *up* at hills whose summits are higher since the original city of Jerusalem was surrounded by mountains. In the same way, God promised to surround His people in order to protect them.

We can rest on this unshakable security because God provides an unbroken wall of protection around us. But we may be asking ourselves, *If God has promised to provide such security and protection, why do bad things occasionally happen to those who are His followers?* From Job, to Jeremiah, to the apostles, many sincere and godly men and women have experienced times of stress and pain.

And that's the key point to note here. The psalmist *isn't* saying that those who follow God will never have problems. Rather, he's saying that those who put their trust in God won't have their faith shaken when times of testing come because God will continue to be with them, even through those difficult times. If we read verse 3 in context, the psalmist is saying that God will continue to uphold His people so that "the scepter of wickedness shall not rest upon the land of the righteous, so that the righteous will not put forth their hands to do wrong." God will keep evil within bounds so that His followers will not lose heart and turn to evil themselves.

The message of this psalm is similar to that of 1 Corinthians 10:13. "No temptation has overtaken you but such as is common to man; and God is faithful, who will not allow you to be tempted beyond what you are able, but with the temptation will provide the way of escape also, so that you will be able to endure it." Trials will come, but they will be regulated by a God who is constantly watching over His followers to make sure they don't become overwhelmed by difficulties.

The psalmist ends the psalm with a concluding wish or prayer to God: "Do good, O Lord, to those who are good and to those who are upright in their hearts" (v. 4). He asks God to bless those who are spiritually and morally upright and to lead away or remove the "doers of iniquity," those causing all the problems.

**WALKING IN OUR LAND**

**WE ALL FACE TIMES** in our lives when it seems as if the only way to get ahead is to cut corners, lower our standards, and go with the flow—because, we're told, only chumps and losers do what's right and play by the rules. During those times of testing we need to lift our spiritual eyes and take a look at God's heavenly horizon. Those who commit to the moral absolutes of God's Word have an anchor that will keep them rock solid in a shifting moral climate.

Equally assuring, they can depend on God's presence and His protection, which are as certain as the mountains surrounding the original city of Jerusalem!

# Our Builder, Protector, and Provider

## PSALM 127

Sometimes the rerelease of a song is more popular than the original. If you've ever watched the 1942 film *Casablanca*, you probably remember Ilsa asking the piano player, "Play it, Sam. Play 'As Time Goes By.'" The song was immortalized by that movie, but you may not know that it was actually written eleven years earlier for the 1931 Broadway musical, *Everybody's Welcome*. It was well-received in the musical, but its enduring popularity came from its reuse in the famous film starring Humphrey Bogart and Ingrid Bergman.

There's a song in the Bible with a similar history. It was originally composed by King Solomon, who was a prolific songwriter. The writer of 1 Kings 4:32 says the king wrote 1,005 songs. Of that large number, only two made it into the book of Psalms, Israel's national songbook. And of those two, one made it as a kind of "rerelease," to be used in a totally different context: Psalm 127.

Our study of this psalm takes us to the crowded city of Jerusalem, which is packed with pilgrims who have gathered to celebrate one of Israel's three annual feasts. The narrow streets are jammed, and people are sleeping wherever they can find room to unroll their blankets. It's a time of excitement, but it's also a time when patience can wear thin and stress increases. And perhaps that's why several of the psalms, including 127, were included in the Songs of Ascents—songs to be sung as the pilgrims ascended to Jerusalem to celebrate one of the holy feasts of the year.

Ten of the fifteen psalms of ascents are anonymous, four were written by David, and one by Solomon. Whatever their original setting, the psalms by David and Solomon were "rereleased" and included as part of this collection, giving them a new significance for the nation. With that in mind, let's look at Psalm 127.

This five-verse psalm has two stanzas and three themes. The first stanza, found in verses 1–2, introduces all three themes. God is our builder, our protector, and our provider. First, He's our *builder*. "Unless the Lord builds the house, they labor in vain who build it" (v. 1a). Perhaps Solomon first wrote this psalm as he was building God's temple, or even his own palace. But since the psalm made its way into this collection, the house became a metaphor for all of life. Success in life usually comes through hard work. But if our work isn't aligned with and supported by God, ultimately it will fail.

Solomon then changes themes as he turns to focus on God as our *protector*. "Unless the LORD guards the city, the watchman keeps awake in vain" (v. 1b). We all seek safety and security. We install locks on our doors and passwords on our computers. Nationally, we spend billions of dollars on defense against possible attacks. But Solomon reminds his readers, including us, that ultimate security comes only from God. Without His protection, we have no real security.

The walls of the old city of Jerusalem at night.

Solomon transitions to his third theme in verse 2. In addition to being our *builder* and our *protector*, God is also our *provider*. "It is vain for you to rise up early, to retire late, to eat the bread of painful labors; for He gives to His beloved even in his sleep." Solomon's words may surprise those familiar with all the proverbs he wrote on the importance of diligence and hard work. But Solomon's words here don't conflict with the message of the book of Proverbs. That book has much to say about the hard work needed to survive in the dawn-to-dusk reality of an agrarian society. Psalm 127 is *not* saying God will allow His followers to become lazy. Instead, Solomon is saying we need to realize that any benefits we receive from our labor ultimately come from God. He is the one who provides everything necessary for the crops to grow, even at night when we're asleep!

In verses 3–5 Solomon changes illustrations, focusing on the blessing of children. But his three main themes remain the same, though he now presents them in reverse order—focusing on God as our *provider*, then our *protector*, and then our *builder*. Let me say right at the beginning that Solomon is *not* writing to say that sons are better than daughters (as a few Bible versions translate verses 3–4). Nor is he making a statement against family planning or birth control, suggesting that God wants parents to have as many children as possible. Rather, Solomon focuses on something highly valued in his culture and uses it as an illustration to remind his readers that God is the ultimate source of blessing.

In a society that attached a high value to large families, Solomon states that even children come from God. "Children are a gift of the LORD; the fruit of the womb is a reward" (v. 3). Lest his listeners be tempted to brag about their large families, Solomon reminds them that God is the ultimate *provider*. Children are *His* gift!

God is also the *protector*. The children God provides are "like arrows in the hand of a warrior" (v. 4). In a culture that viewed large families as a means of safety and protection, a man with many children was like a warrior going into battle with a full quiver of arrows. But Solomon reminded his readers that even this protection ultimately comes from God. Remember, "children are a *gift of the LORD*" (italics added).

Solomon ends his psalm by stressing again the theme he used at the very beginning: God is our *builder*, the One who advances our cause and guarantees our success. And those who have been blessed by God with children "will not be ashamed when they speak with their enemies in the gate." Being blessed by God doesn't mean we will never face opposition or obstacles. The gates of a city functioned as the courthouse of the day, and Solomon is envisioning a scene in which a righteous person has been falsely accused by his enemies. But because his children are able to stand beside him as both his witnesses and his allies, he doesn't have to face the opposition alone. God's provision of children helps assure success.

**WALKING IN OUR LAND**

**THOSE SINGING THESE TRUTHS** as they approached Jerusalem—that God provides, protects, and advances their cause—were reminded of a more fundamental truth about God. It's a truth we should remember as well. God is the source of ultimate success in life. Sadly, too many Christians today live as functional atheists, paying lip service to God but acting as if success depends on their efforts alone. Solomon wants us to remember that God is our builder, our protector, and our provider. To think otherwise is foolish—and dangerous.

So how dependent are you on God? This might be a good time to take stock of your life. Make sure God is indeed *your* builder, protector, and provider.

# Like Father, Like Son

## PSALM 131

We've all heard the expression, "The apple doesn't fall far from the tree." The reality behind that expression is the fact that parents' character traits often show up in their children. The phrase itself has been around since the sixteenth century and speaks to the truth that family characteristics often get passed along to our offspring. Sometimes it can be physical characteristics like the color of the eyes or the contours of the face. Other times it can be specific mannerisms, facial expressions, or even patterns of speech. But is this expression also true in the spiritual realm? David seems to suggest that it is in Psalm 131, a psalm of childlike trust.

Though Psalm 131 lists David as its author, it was not included with most of his other psalms at the beginning of the book. Instead, this psalm was added to the Songs of Ascents. Psalm 131 is deceptively simple and is a short, three-verse psalm that can easily be overlooked as we hurriedly try to read through our Bible. But the message is profound, which might be why the psalm was placed in this collection. Let's slow down to look more closely at this psalm of trust.

David began by affirming his humility before God. "O LORD, my heart is not proud, nor my eyes haughty." Pride is an oft-repeated sin in the Bible. It led to Satan's rebellion against God. When Satan tempted Adam and Eve, the core of his offer was that they could become like God. The book of Proverbs often reminded Israel of the danger of pride. "Pride goes before destruction, and a haughty spirit before stumbling" (16:18). Pride is an inflated view of one's self-importance and self-sufficiency that says, "I don't need God's help. I'm good enough to do it myself!"

David lets his readers know he isn't self-sufficient! In fact, he finishes this first verse by focusing on his humble spirit, which is the opposite of pride. "Nor do I involve myself in great matters, or in things too difficult for me." It's important to understand what David is *not* saying here. He is not suggesting that ignorance is bliss or that we shouldn't strive to learn and grow and develop in maturity. Rather, he has in view those aspects of life that he knows are out of his control. Rather than boasting about

An Israeli soldier holding his child in his arms.

his own abilities, David is willing to humbly acknowledge that the God of Israel is God, while he—David—is not.

Instead of claiming to be the master of his fate and the captain of his soul, David begins by acknowledging that there's much in life that is simply beyond his understanding. He humbly accepts God's sovereign control, but that doesn't mean David sees himself as a passive blob of humanity being swept helplessly through life. He does speak to the key role he plays in his relationship to God, and it's much harder to accomplish than it might seem. He describes that role in verse 2, "Surely I have composed and quieted my soul; like a weaned child rests against his mother, my soul is like a weaned child within me."

The picture David paints is that of a child who is just

beyond the infant and toddler stages. Infants are adorable, but they're also incredibly demanding and still have many needs that must be met by their parents. David deliberately chooses the imagery of a slightly older child, one who has been weaned. In David's day a child could be breastfed until he or she was about three years old. A child at that age is older, more mature, and more capable of self-control. More than that, a three-year-old is at a magical age, possessing a sense of wonder, childlike faith, and trust. David's task in life is to develop a childlike trust in God, a trust that will keep him close to God with a spirit that's content.

David focused his efforts on developing the kind of trust in God that a child instinctively has in his mother. And then in the final verse of this brief psalm, David takes this truth and applies it to his audience. "O Israel, hope in the LORD from this time forth and forever." The word for "hope" conveys the idea of waiting with a sense of expectation, similar to the way a child might behave after asking his or her mother for a glass of water—waiting patiently but expectantly.

Notice that this final verse bears a striking resemblance to the next-to-last verse of the previous psalm. "O Israel, hope in the LORD; for with the LORD there is lovingkindness, and with Him is abundant redemption"

(130:7). Psalm 130 tells us *why* we should wait expectantly for God, because of His loyal love and plentiful redemption. Psalm 131 tells us *how* to wait on God—with the innocent trust of a young child.

### WALKING IN OUR LAND

**JESUS WAS THE ULTIMATE SON** who displayed unswerving trust in His Father in every circumstance, humbling Himself to the point where He was willing to say, "not My will, but Yours be done" (Luke 22:42). David tried hard to be the same sort of humble, obedient son, and he ended the psalm by calling on us to follow in his footsteps. Pride (the attitude that I can do it all myself) and impatience (thinking I want it all now) bring us into conflict with God . . . while humility and a sense of patient trust place us in the proper relationship to Him.

Jesus is our ultimate example. Remember . . . like Father, like Son. We too can trust in God during our journey through life. Have "hope" in Him, waiting with a sense of expectation for Him to lead—and then follow in His path.

# The Blessings of Unity

## PSALM 133

There's an old Irish toast to family and friends that contains more than its share of truth:

To live above with the Saints we love,
Ah, that is the purest glory.
To live below with the Saints we know,
Ah, that is another story![1]

This saying always comes to my mind on about the fifth day of a trip to Israel! Jet lag has worn off, we're all settled in, and our days and nights are now in sync. Yet this is when we notice a few members of the group who seem to be getting on everyone's nerves. They're the ones who are *always* five minutes late getting back on the bus . . . at every stop! They hold everyone else up in the dinner line as they examine each piece of lettuce in the salad before putting it on their plate!

Why is it that people's idiosyncrasies only seem to show up when we get together in groups? And why do such small irritations upset us so much? I'm glad our destination today is Mount Hermon because I think this location can help us answer that question.

Mount Hermon rises 9,200 feet above sea level. It's the highest mountain in Israel. The cities of Dan and Caesarea Philippi are nestled at the base of Mount Hermon, but you can't get a good view of the mountain from either site. They're just too close. So let's stop by the ancient city of Hazor for a better view. Mount Hermon is

A view of snow-capped Mount Hermon from the ancient town of Hazor.

still thirty miles away, but from here we can see how the mountain dominates the view to the north.

But what does majestic Mount Hermon have to do with the always-late lettuce-inspector now sitting in front of you on the bus? To find the answer we need to visit Jerusalem during one of the annual feasts of the Lord. Imagine having to crowd into the city of Jerusalem with this person—and thousands of others—three times each year as we gather as a nation before the Lord! It's supposed to be a time of spiritual inspiration, but it would have been easy to become overcome with irritation!

I believe that's why Psalm 133 was included among the Songs of Ascents. Originally written by David, this psalm focuses on the benefits of brotherly unity, and David uses Mount Hermon as one of his object lessons. David may have written the psalm after he was made king, ending a period of civil war among the tribes. But whatever its original background, the later compilers included it as part of this group of psalms sung by the thousands of pilgrims ascending to Jerusalem to worship the Lord.

The psalm begins with a simple declaration: "Behold, how good and how pleasant it is for brothers to dwell together in unity!" Simply dwelling together wasn't the goal. Rather, the goal was to dwell together in unity of purpose and heart. Such unity, David writes, is both morally good and socially agreeable. Unity is always right from God's perspective, and it's what keeps the fabric of society from unraveling.

David then uses two examples to illustrate the benefits of such unity. First he compares the benefits of true unity to the oil Moses poured on Aaron's head when he anointed him to be high priest. "It is like the precious oil upon the head, coming down upon the beard, even Aaron's beard, coming down upon the edge of his robes" (v. 2). In Exodus 40 God announced that Aaron and his sons were to be set apart to "a perpetual priesthood throughout their generations" (v. 15). That happened when Moses "poured some of the anointing oil on Aaron's head and anointed him, to consecrate him" (Lev. 8:12).

As the fragrant anointing oil ran down Aaron's head onto his beard, and then dripped onto his priestly garments, he was *sanctified*—set apart to God in a unique and special way. David is saying that as we live together in unity, each of us helps draw one another closer to the Lord. How does this work? The writer of Hebrews suggests it happens as we encourage and support one another in our walk with God. "Let us consider how to stimulate one another to love and good deeds, not forsaking our own assembling together, as is the habit of some, but encouraging one another; and all the more as you see the day drawing near" (Heb. 10:24–25). Being together, encouraging each other, and demonstrating love and practical concern. In these ways we help draw one another closer to God. These are the *sanctifying effects* of brotherly unity.

David then illustrates in verse 3 the *sustaining effect* that brotherly unity can have on us, keeping us going during the difficult times in our lives. It's here where he takes his readers on a majestic sweep of Israel, from Mount Hermon in the north to Mount Zion in the south. Brotherly unity is like "the dew of Hermon coming down upon the mountains of Zion." David's illustration is drawn from the dry summer months when no rain falls in Israel. On most summer days a warm, moist breeze blows in from off the Mediterranean. In the evening, when the sun goes down and the warmth radiates away into the clear night sky, the temperature can drop below the dew point, especially in the higher elevations. Though Mount Hermon receives a great deal of rain in the winter, it is the summer dew that helps nourish and sustain the trees and bushes that grow on its slopes throughout the dry season.

In the same way, brotherly unity has a sustaining effect on those who experience it. It's as if, David says, the heavy dew from Mount Hermon could also fall on the lower heights of Mount Zion, bringing the moisture to sustain it through the dry summer. Just as God brought the physical dew to the heights of Mount Hermon, so He promised to bring His "blessing" on those who gathered to worship Him in Jerusalem.

**WALKING IN OUR LAND**

**OUR TIME AT MOUNT HERMON** is one not only of beauty but also of practicality. The annoying dryness of summer is a reminder that there are seasons when refreshing rains and snows that offer sustenance are replaced by times of spiritual barrenness. Yet in those times even a light dew is helpful. "The dew of Hermon" plays a vital role in sustaining life during the dry summer months, and so do the people whom God brings into our lives. They all help us grow into people of God. In an age of text messages and tweets, we're often in danger of substituting impersonal communication for personal interaction, perhaps letting our social media posts replace actual face time with friends and family and, yes, even casual acquaintances whom God brings into our lives. When we let these conveniences substitute for our personal interactions, we can become spiritually impoverished, and the strong bonds of unity can be frayed.

So don't forsake the gathering together in unity that is both sanctifying and sustaining—even with the always-late lettuce-inspectors in your life. See if you can get together for a meal, and ask about their spiritual journey. You might discover that the lessons God is teaching them can help you in your spiritual walk. God just might use them to draw you closer to Him and encourage you in your walk of faith. Remember, it's good and pleasant when *all* believers dwell together in unity!

# Night Shift

## PSALM 134

When I was in high school, I had a friend who worked for a while as a night watchman at a local textile company. One night I drove to the mill to visit Danny and walked with him as he made one of his hourly rounds through the factory. That was the first time I ever saw a night watchman's clock or watch clock—a clock with a leather case and a key slot at one end. As we walked the floors, Danny would stop at different spots and insert a key that was hanging there into the clock, which would then record the time he visited that location.

That clock served a very useful purpose. The job of the night watchman was to guard and protect the building when nobody else was around. But who was there to make sure the night watchman didn't take a little siesta himself? The night watchman's clock was really designed to make sure the night watchman was awake and patrolling the factory on a regular schedule. It helped keep him faithful at a time when no one else was around to check up on him.

And that got me thinking: what would it have been like to work the night shift at the Temple in Jerusalem? In his book, *The Temple—Its Ministry and Services*,[1] Alfred Edersheim helps provide the answer. He described the many activities that took place during the evening in the Temple. The worshipers were gone, the massive doors were closed, but the work continued. The entire complex had to be guarded. The menorah had to be kept lit, its bowls filled with olive oil, and its wicks trimmed. The courtyards needed to be cleaned and all the funds collected the previous day had to be counted. The wood for the altar of sacrifice had to be replenished, and the animals for the next day's sacrifice had to be selected.

There was much to do, and the work couldn't be outsourced. It had to be done by the priests and Levites. So imagine you're a priest assigned to the night shift at the Temple. You report to work just as the evening sacrifice is being offered and as the final worshipers are preparing to leave and head home. The job might be exciting for the first day or two, but then reality sets in. It's dark at night, and often cold. It's hard to work all night and then try to sleep during the day. All the energy that comes from ministering before the daily visitors is missing. Who really cares if you're in charge of filling the oil lamps on the menorah at midnight? God may have commanded Aaron and his sons to "keep [the lamp] in order from evening to morning before the LORD" (Ex. 27:21), but it wasn't a glamorous job!

And that's why I love Psalm 134, the final psalm of the fifteen arranged together into the Songs of Ascents. This psalm concludes the pilgrims' time in Jerusalem as they get ready to head back to their homes. The psalm itself is very short, a mere three verses. Yet it has an important message for those working the night shift, those

The sunset from Jerusalem.

serving sometimes alone, often with little recognition, and typically without appreciation.

The psalm is a psalm of blessing, and it's divided into two parts, each having a different speaker and audience. In verses 1–2 the people of Israel are the ones speaking, and their words are addressed to the priests, specifically to the priests going on night duty. These two verses begin and end with the people calling on these priests to "bless the LORD."

This doesn't mean the priests were being asked to somehow impart a special blessing to God. God is already perfect, and we can't add to His perfection. When the word "bless" is used with reference to God, it's referring to our act of worship or adoration. The word can also mean "to kneel," and it's in that sense that we bless God as we adore Him on bended knee, so to speak, acknowledging His supreme glory and greatness.

The people identified these priests as "servants of the LORD" and as those who "serve by night in the house of the LORD." As the crowds leave to go home, the priests on the night shift begin their work that's not in the public eye, which might seem less glamorous. But the worshipers' parting words remind these priests that their ministry is to the God of the universe. That's who they're serving, that's who they're standing before all night, and that's who they're seeking to worship and adore through their actions.

It's almost as if the crowd is foreshadowing Paul's words to the believing slaves in the city of Ephesus, where Paul called on them to serve "not by way of eye-service, as men-pleasers, but as slaves of Christ, doing the will of God from the heart. With good will render service, as to the Lord, and not to men" (Eph. 6:6–7). In the same way, the people now leaving Jerusalem call on the priests to continue serving God even at night, when others aren't around to see or voice appreciation for what they're doing.

Then in the final verse of the psalm the priests return the favor, calling on God to bless the departing crowd. "May the LORD bless you from Zion, He who made heaven and earth" (v. 3). The priests use the same word for "bless," but now, as the mediators between God and the people, they're asking God to extend His blessing to the people. The pilgrims might be heading home from Mount Zion, but the priests are asking God to bless them on their journey.

**WALKING IN OUR LAND**

**THIS SHORT PSALM** reminds us that no task is menial if it's done to serve God. Whether it's filling the temple lamps with oil in the middle of the night—or changing diapers in the church nursery—if we're serving God, then our work has significance. Even if others don't see or appreciate what we're doing, God does.

The other truth we can take away is that we need to pause intentionally and show appreciation to those who are serving the Lord in obscure ways. This coming Sunday, stop by the church nursery or Sunday school classrooms and tell all the workers how much you appreciate them. Walk up to the custodian, parking attendant, or greeter and tell them how much you appreciate their service for Christ.

Remember, the gift of gratitude is one gift you can give that enriches others without ever impoverishing you!

# Repetition and Review

## PSALM 136

I once had a teacher who said the secret to effective communication is repetition and review. Tell people what you're going to say. Then say it. Then tell them what you said. And that's exactly what the writer of Psalm 136 must have had in mind as he composed his ultimate psalm of thanksgiving to God.

Psalm 136 totals twenty-six verses in our Bibles, but it quickly becomes clear that the psalmist wants to drive home just two key points using repetition and review. His first point focuses on *what* he wants his audience to do. Verse 1: "Give thanks to the LORD." Verse 2: "Give thanks to the God of gods." Verse 3: "Give thanks to the Lord of lords." And lest you miss the point, he comes back to review this first key point in the final verse. "Give thanks to the God of heaven." So *what* does he want us to do? He wants us to pause and give thanks to God!

But that raises a question: *Why* should we be so thankful to God? And the writer provides us with an answer as he makes his second point, again using repetition and review to drive home the message. In verse 1 he says we should be thankful because God is "good." The Hebrew word for "good," *tov*, is used in a broad sense throughout the Old Testament to describe something that is pleasing, pleasant, delicious, agreeable, kind, or beneficial. When used to describe God, the foundational idea of *tov* is His moral goodness. The writer is saying we should be thankful to God just because His essential nature is good. The Bible tells us that God is loving, just, merciful,

Looking out over the rugged hills around Mount Sinai.

kind, honest, truthful, and dependable. All of those characteristics make Him "good."

But we're not just to thank God for who He is. The writer also explains—twenty-six times to be exact!—that we're to thank God for *what He has done*. Every single verse in this psalm ends exactly the same way: "For His lovingkindness is everlasting." We know God is good because He has continually demonstrated His loyal love to His followers through the ages.

Since the psalmist uses this phrase in every verse, let's make sure we understand exactly what it means. The word for "lovingkindness" is *hesed*, and it's one of the most amazing words in the Hebrew Bible. It certainly indicates goodness and kindness, but the word means much, much more. It's connected with fidelity: the willingness to faithfully stick by commitments. It carries the idea of extending help to the lowly and less fortunate. And, the psalmist says, God will keep demonstrating His loyal love "forever" (literally, "unto the ages"). Long after the Energizer Bunny has stopped banging on his drum, God's faithful love and care will keep going and going!

But how do we know God's lovingkindness is everlasting? The psalmist takes his readers on an extended journey through history to prove his point. By reading the first line of every verse beginning with verse 5 you can follow the psalmist's sweep of history. In verses 5–9 he traces God's amazing power in creation. From the fashioning of the heavens through the forming of the sun, moon, and stars, God faithfully designed the perfect universe for humanity.

In verses 10–15 the psalmist traces God's loyal love to Israel as He delivered them from Egypt "with a strong hand and an outstretched arm" (v. 12). God "divided the Red Sea asunder" and then "overthrew Pharaoh and his army" in the same body of water (vv. 13, 15). God had promised Abraham that He would bring His descendants out of Egypt (Gen. 15:13–14), and God faithfully kept His word.

The psalmist summarizes the entire forty years in the desert in verse 16, declaring that God "led His people through the wilderness." He then highlights the conquest of the Promised Land in verses 17–22. God "smote great kings" (v. 17) and "gave their land as a heritage" (v. 21). In just eighteen verses the writer shares a panoramic overview of history—from creation through the conquest.

And then, lest anyone somehow still miss his point, this master teacher once again uses repetition and review. In the final four verses he summarizes everything he's just said—doing so in reverse order! Verses 23–24: Don't forget what God has done for Israel. He "remembered us in our low estate" and "rescued us from our adversaries." Verse 25: And remember how He was thinking of us even as He planned creation. He "gives food to all flesh." And then finally in verse 26: So what is it we ought to do as a result? "Give thanks to the God of heaven, for His lovingkindness is everlasting."

Don't forget to thank God for His loyal love when you pray!

**WALKING IN OUR LAND**

**EVERY YEAR** the United States sets aside the fourth Thursday in November as a time to give thanks to God. Canada sets aside the second Monday in October as day of national thanksgiving. But as followers of God we ought to be thankful *every* day of the year. We should thank God for who He is as well as for all the blessings He has poured out on us. But sometimes, when life is difficult, we can find it hard to respond to God with thankful hearts. And that's exactly when the secret of repetition and review from Psalm 136 can become so helpful.

Take out a sheet of paper or grab a notebook and write down all the descriptions of God you can think of. He's the Creator, the Good Shepherd, the One who calms the wind and the waves. That very short list will help you get started. The key is to focus on God and what the Bible says about Him. Then on another sheet, write down all the times in your life when God has answered your prayers, met your needs, or resolved your problems. Try to be as specific as you can—names, dates, and places!

Now read through both lists one line at a time. After each line, pause and say to yourself, "For His lovingkindness is everlasting." Repetition and review. It's a helpful way to master information . . . and to put life in perspective!

# The Legs of a Man

## PSALM 147

The late Dr. J. Dwight Pentecost, distinguished Bible professor from Dallas Theological Seminary, had the look of an Old Testament prophet. Dr. P, as he was known to all, tried to present a persona that was serious, almost stern. He was the Christian Billy Goat Gruff. But deep down the man was a marshmallow. He had a servant's heart and a great sense of humor.

But I admit that I was taken aback during one trip to Israel with Dr. P when someone asked him if he was planning to wear short pants. I tried to picture the venerable Dr. P in shorts, but my mind drew a blank. Dr. Pentecost shocked me back to reality with his quick-witted response to our fellow participant: "[God] delighteth not . . . in the legs of a man!" (Ps. 147:10 KJV). I had to go to my Bible concordance for that one. And that's when I discovered Psalm 147.

To understand this psalm I want you to follow me as we walk *up, up, up* the Mount of Olives. Okay, we've reached the top. How do your legs feel? If they feel like rubber, you're not alone. I know there are some who can sprint to the top and barely break a sweat, but *most* of us find it to be a fairly difficult hike. Now that we've reached the top, turn and look at Jerusalem. Picture a temple standing where the Dome of the Rock now sits. That's the view you need to have in front of you as we begin our study of this psalm!

Psalm 147 begins and ends with the same command: "Praise the LORD!" In Hebrew the word is *Hallelujah*, which means to shout out in praise, almost to the point of boasting. And who is it that we are to be shouting/praising/boasting about? It's *Yah*, a shortened form of Yahweh, the covenant-keeping God of Israel. The God whose visible presence is represented by that temple down below.

The psalm is divided into three stanzas, each of which begins with a call to praise God. We've seen that call in verse 1. Now look at the beginning of the second stanza in verse 7. "Sing to the LORD with thanksgiving." And then again in stanza three that begins with, "Praise the LORD, O Jerusalem!" (v. 12). The city is instructed and called to boast about God, to shout out and sing His

Looking down on Jerusalem and the Dome of the Rock from atop the Mount of Olives.

praises. But what is it about God that's motivation for such thanksgiving? To answer that, let's look more closely at the three stanzas. Each one follows a similar pattern. The psalmist first gives the *call* to praise, and then he follows by sharing the *cause* for praise, the reason we're to be so thankful to God.

In verses 1–6 we're to praise God because of His amazing deeds. In verse 2 we learn that God "builds up Jerusalem" and "gathers the outcasts of Israel." The psalmist is describing the regathering of the people and the rebuilding of Jerusalem and the Temple, likely following the Babylonian exile. That's when God brought

His people back from captivity. The writer describes the exile as if it were a deep gash in the very soul of the Jewish people, and he joyfully announces that God "heals the brokenhearted and binds up their wounds" (v. 3).

But then the psalmist makes what appears to be a very dramatic leap in logic. The God who restored His people is the very God who controls the universe itself. He "counts the number of the stars; He gives names to all of them" (v. 4). But why did the psalmist shift topics to begin talking about God's control over the stars in the sky? It was a reminder that the God who did the impossible for them could do so because He is also a God who is "abundant in strength" and whose "understanding is infinite" (v. 5). We can be thankful because the God who set in motion and controls the universe is the same God who stoops to help those in need.

In the second stanza, verses 7–11, the psalmist continues this theme. After calling on the people to sing with thanksgiving, he explains how God meets our needs in mysterious ways. God "covers the heavens with clouds," "provides rain for the earth," and "makes grass grow on the mountains" (v. 8). God also "gives to the beast its food, and to the young ravens which cry" (v. 9). At first, this focus on God's control over weather and care for even the ravens seems to make no sense, but follow the psalmist's reasoning. God shifts the clouds . . . which bring rain . . . which causes grass to grow . . . which feeds the animals. We might not fully understand why God works the way He does. But *He* understands every detail of life, even to the point that life's literal and figurative storms serve a necessary purpose.

And *this* is where the psalmist inserts the verse that Dr. Pentecost quoted! "He does not delight in the strength of the horse; He takes no pleasure in the legs of a man" (v. 10 NKJV). But of course this verse is *not* really referring to wearing short pants! The writer is asking what delights a God of such amazing wisdom and power. It's not the things we might think of as powerful. The horse was the fastest of the animals man could control, and our legs are the most powerful part of our body. But God isn't impressed with those things that often impress us. Instead, the psalmist says, God "takes pleasure in those who fear Him, in those who hope in his steadfast love" (v. 11 NRSV). God esteems those who focus not on their own strength but who instead recognize their dependence on Him!

The final stanza of this psalm is found in verses 12–20. The writer calls on the people to thank God for His protection and His blessing. Jerusalem might have been rebuilt, but the city still needed to remember that it was

God who "strengthened the bars of your gates" (v. 13). Ultimately it was God, and God alone, who could make "peace in your borders" (v. 14).

For a third time the psalmist uses an unusual comparison to drive home his point—this time pointing to the violent weather God can unleash on the earth. "He gives snow like wool; he scatters frost like ashes. He hurls down hail like crumbs—who can stand before his cold?" (vv. 16–17 NRSV). Having grown up in the northeastern United States, I have vivid memories of the cold, snow, and ice God can send on the earth. But the God who can send trouble like hail raining down from the sky is also the God who "sends out his word, and melts them" (v. 18 NRSV).

Having mentioned God's commands to nature, the writer ends by remembering the written Word God has also given to His people. "He declares his word to Jacob, his statutes and ordinances to Israel" (v. 19 NRSV). The God of the universe has graciously shared His written word with Israel and, by extension, with His followers today.

**WALKING IN OUR LAND**

**SO WHAT CAN WE LEARN** from Psalm 147? I think we can learn how to praise God. We praise God because of His unsurpassed greatness and power—which He uses to care for His children. We praise Him because He understands the complexities of life in a way that allows Him to work all things together for good to meet the needs of His followers (see Rom. 8:28). We praise Him because His amazing work through nature is eclipsed by what He has revealed to us in His Word.

God doesn't delight in the legs of a man, but He does take great delight in those followers who submit to Him in reverential awe, in those who look to Him to meet their needs, who trust in Him through life's uncertainties, and who humbly seek to read and obey His Word!

# Strike Up the Band

## PSALM 150

If I say "Strike Up the Band," what comes to mind? If you're a music buff, you might think of George and Ira Gershwin. They composed the tune and lyrics of this song in 1927 for a musical by the same name. But if you're a movie buff, you might remember the 1940 MGM film with the same title starring Judy Garland and Mickey Rooney.

If you attended UCLA, the name could conjure up images of home football games and the Bruins' marching band strutting across midfield at halftime. The Gershwins donated the "Strike Up the Band" tune to UCLA, and it's been part of the school's musical history ever since.

But whichever image comes to mind, it's likely you're now thinking about a lively tune with a full band or orchestra thump, thump, thumping its way through your brain.

But I'm almost certain you *didn't* think of the final

song in Israel's songbook—though "Strike Up the Band" is what the author of Psalm 150 might have wanted to name his composition!

Each of the five individual "books" that make up the entire book of Psalms ends with a call to praise God. Psalm 41 completes the first collection of psalms, and it ends with these words: "Blessed be the Lord, the God of Israel, from everlasting to everlasting. Amen and Amen" (v. 13). A similar call to praise is found at the end of Psalms 72, 89, and 106—the last psalms in Books II, III, and IV. But what's a fitting ending for the *entire* book of Psalms? What kind of exclamation point can God place at the end of this amazing work?

A harpist greeting visitors inside Jaffa Gate in Jerusalem.

It requires more than just a phrase, or a verse—or even an entire psalm. The last *five* psalms—Psalms 146 through 150—are the ending call to praise for the complete book of Psalms. In these five songs the book reaches its crescendo. Today we're heading back to Jerusalem to listen to the final chorus in God's call to praise. So grab your sweater and camera as we head to the hill west of Jerusalem for tonight's performance.

The theme for tonight's concert is impossible to miss. Each of the final five psalms begins and ends with the same Hebrew phrase: *Hallelujah* . . . praise the LORD! The main focus is on God. He is deserving of our praise. After spending so much time over the past month of our devotional meditations focusing on our needs, our concerns, and our problems, now it's time for God to take center stage. Unfortunately, all too often we forget but, really, that should be our constant focus.

The writer begins by telling us *where* we are to praise God. "Praise God in His sanctuary; praise Him in His mighty expanse" (v. 1). Certainly the Temple in Jerusalem was the place where God summoned Israel to worship Him. "Then it shall come about that the place in which the LORD your God will choose for His name to dwell, there you shall bring all that I command you. . . . And you shall rejoice before the LORD your God" (Deut. 12:11–12).

But even as he was dedicating the Temple to God, Solomon recognized that a mere structure here on earth—even one as grand as the one he had built—couldn't contain or limit the God of the universe. "But will God indeed dwell on the earth? Behold, heaven and the highest heaven cannot contain You, how much less this house which I have built!" (1 Kings 8:27). Perhaps that's why the psalmist moves from the "sanctuary" to God's "mighty expanse." The grandeur of the limitless starry heavens is a more fitting canopy under which to praise the limitless God of the universe.

After telling us *where* to praise God, the writer then describes *why* we are to praise Him. "Praise Him for His mighty deeds; praise Him according to His excellent greatness" (v. 2). Praise God for *what* He has done and for *who* He is. The size of our problems is always in inverse proportion to the greatness of our God. Big God, small problems. Small God, big problems. Praise Him for being such a great God!

The next three verses form the largest section of this final psalm. This is where the writer tells us *how* to praise God. It's here that he tells us to strike up the band! And what a band it is! His orchestra includes a brass section, strings, woodwinds, and percussion. It also includes a chorus line . . . or at least a section with dancers. The

Hebrew word for dancing (v. 4) comes from a root word that conveys the idea of swirling or turning. In a few contexts it's translated as whirlwind. You definitely get the idea of energy, passion, and movement. This parade is heading down Main Street—and the twirlers are part of the marching band!

We now know *where* to praise God, *why* to praise Him, and *how* to praise. But *who* is included in this original "praise band"? The psalmist provides the answer in the final verse: "Let everything that has breath praise the LORD." I like the requirement for being part of this musical group. You don't need to know how to play an instrument or even how to sing or dance. The *only* requirement is that you must be breathing. If you're alive, then you qualify! No other experience is necessary!

The psalmist ends the psalm—and the book—with one final command: "Praise the LORD!" (v. 6). *Hallelujah*! *You* need to praise God! And that's a fitting way for us to end our thirty-day journey through the land of Israel with David and the other psalmists.

**WALKING IN OUR LAND**

**HOW GREAT IS YOUR GOD?** Remember, "The size of our problems is always in inverse proportion to the greatness of our God." When you realize you have a big God, your problems become smaller. Praise Him today for being such a great God! Praise God for *what* He has done and for *who* He is.

As we get ready to say our goodbyes and part company, let me ask two final questions. During this time together, what key truths did you learn about God? What lessons did you learn about your daily walk with Him? The images of the land will eventually fade like the photographs of long-ago journeys. And the message of the individual psalms might grow dim. But your walk with God can remain strong if you remember His awesome power, His deep love for you . . . and your need to stay close to Him.

None of us knows how long we will march in this parade we call life. But the best way to keep from stumbling and falling is to face forward and keep our eyes focused on Jesus as we continue to praise the Father and the Son. And as you march, step along with a song in your heart and a smile on your lips! Remember, "Let everything that has breath praise the Lord!"

# Notes

## Introduction

1. Warren W. Wiersbe, *Be Worshipful (Psalms 1–89)* (Colorado Springs: Victor, 2004), 15.

## Day 3: God Is My Masada

1. Josephus, *Wars of the Jews* (7.8.4).

## Day 8: David's Hanukkah Prayer

1. This phrase derives from the poem "Invictus" by William Ernest Henley, in which he writes, "I am the master of my fate, / I am the captain of my soul."

## Day 9: Where Is God When It Hurts?

1. The words of "The Weaver" have been printed in *The Pacific*, vol. 55, October 20, 1915, p. 81, and a portion appeared in *British Books in Print*, 1910, vol. 2, in "Bagster's Quotation Cards." Still earlier the poem was printed in *The American Farmer*, August 1892. Various authors have been credited, including Florence May Alt, John Branister Tabb, and Grant Colfax Tullar. After summarizing the uncertain authorship, Library of Congress reference specialist Abby Yochelson concludes, "It is clear that this poem was published before 1923, putting it in the public domain." See "Lyrics Whodunnit," March 23, 2015, at http://www.theworshipbook.com/blog/lyrics-whodunnit

**Day 14: A Song from the Wilderness**

1. Verse 1, "Only One Life," by C. T. Studd, no date. In public domain.

**Day 15: Under His Wings**

1. From verse 1; William Cushing, "Under His Wings" *Worship and Service Hymnal* (Chicago: Hope Publishing, 1957), 292. In public domain.

**Day 17: The "Old Hundredth"**

1. Thomas Ken, "Praise God from Whom All Blessings Flow" (the Doxology), *Inspiring Hymns* (1709; repr., Chicago: Singspiration, 1951). Ken wrote the original hymn in 1674; one phrase was modified to the current version in 1709. In the public domain. See also James D. Smith III, "Where Did We Get the Doxology?" *Church History;* http://www.christianitytoday.com/history/issues/issue-31/where-did-we-get-doxology.html

**Day 21: A Disturbing Question with a Reassuring Answer**

1. Milded Leightner Dillon, "Safe Am I." Copyright 1938 by William Dillon. Used by permission.

**Day 22: The Peace of Jerusalem**

1. Mark Twain, *The Innocents Abroad* (Hartford: American Publishing Co., 1869; repr. Hertfordshire: Wordsworth Editions, 2010), 303.

**Day 26: The Blessings of Unity**

1. Irish Toasts: "Irish Toasts to Friends & Family"; http://www.islandireland.com/Pages/folk/sets/toasts.html

**Day 27: Night Shift**

1. Alfred Edersheim, *The Temple—Its Ministry and Services as They Were at the Time of Jesus Christ* (London: The Religious Tract Society, 1874). Edersheim devoted an entire chapter ("At Night in the Temple") to this subject.

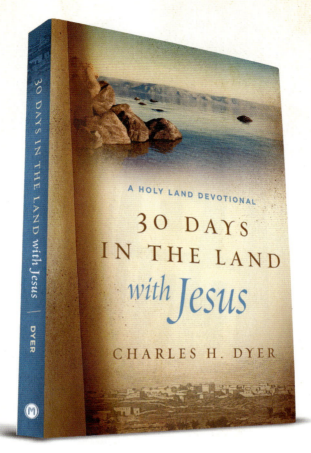

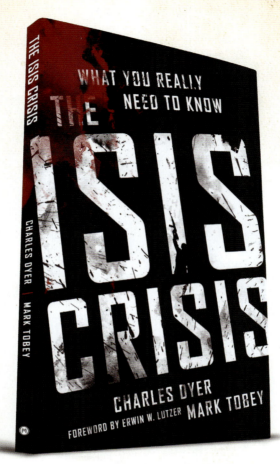

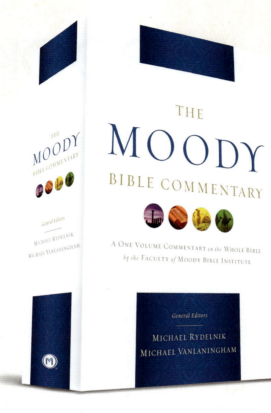

# the LAND and the BOOK

### with Dr. Charlie Dyer

Dr. Charlie Dyer provides biblical insight into the complex tapestry of people and events that make up Israel and the Middle East. Each week he presents an in-depth look at biblical, historical, archeological, and prophetic events and their relevance for today.

**www.thelandandthebook.org**

**MOODY**
**Radio**

*From the Word to Life*